Marie-Dominique Chenu, O.P.

*Translated from the French
by Paul Philibert, O.P.*

Aquinas

and His Role in Theology

A Michael Glazier Book

THE LITURGICAL PRESS
Collegeville, Minnesota

www.litpress.org

A Michael Glazier Book published by Liturgical Press

Cover design by David Manahan, O.S.B. Image detail: *The Triumph of Thomas Aquinas,* anonymous, Church of St. Catherine, Pisa, Italy, 14th c.

This book was first published in French as *St. Thomas d'Aquin et la théologie* by Les Editions du Seuil, © Editions du Seuil, 1959. All rights reserved.

ISBN 13: 978-0-8146-5079-0
ISBN 10: 0-8146-5079-1

3   4   5   6   7   8

Library of Congress Cataloging-in-Publication Data
Chenu, Marie-Dominique, 1895–
    [St. Thomas d'Aquin et la théologie. English]
    Aquinas and his role in theology / Marie Dominique Chenu ; translated from the French by Paul Philibert.
       p. cm.
    "A Michael Glazier book".
    Includes bibliographical references and index.
    ISBN 0-8146-5079-1 (alk. paper)
    1. Thomas, Aquinas, Saint, 1225?–1274. I. Title.

BX4700.T6 C4713 2002
230'.2'092—dc21
                                                    2002071062

Contents

Laus Deo,
Doctori Angelico gratias,
gaudium beato Mariae-Dominico,
mentibusque lectorum pax.

Translator's Introduction

Through the centuries, St. Thomas Aquinas (ca. 1225–74) has been considered a key thinker for Catholic theology. He was canonized in 1323, just fifty years after his death; declared a Doctor of the Church in 1567; and proposed as a model exponent of Catholic theology by Pope Leo XIII in 1879. *Aquinas and His Role in Theology* is an important book by one of the greatest contemporary interpreters of St. Thomas Aquinas. Chenu himself said: "It is possibly the best thing that I have written," most likely because he felt that here he had expressed his feelings for Aquinas more fully than in other, more erudite writings.[1] It is curious, therefore, that this rather small book has not been translated into English before this. But the intervening years since its publication in French in 1959 have done nothing to diminish its relevance. In fact, the reintroduction of Chenu's voice into today's discourse about Aquinas's theology is important, in my view, precisely because of the extraordinary range of his perspectives on Aquinas.

As a young Dominican, Chenu completed his doctorate in Rome in 1920 with a dissertation entitled "A Psychological and Theological Analysis of Contemplation," directed by the reputed Dominican theologian Garrigou-Lagrange. Following that, Chenu was appointed professor at the Saulchoir (the *studium* or seminary for the Paris Dominicans located first in Belgium and then later near Paris). At the same time he became a member of the Historical Institute of Thomistic Studies founded by Pierre Mandonnet, O.P. With his colleagues at the institute, Chenu became a pioneer in medieval studies just as this discipline was becoming significant as a result of the

---

[1] Cf. Jean Jolivet, "Les Études consacrées par le Père Chenu au Moyen Âge," in *Marie-Dominique Chenu: Moyen Âge et Modernité: Les Cahiers du Centre d'études du Saulchoir*, V (Paris: Cerf, 1997) 80.

scholarly work of Étienne Gilson. In 1930, in cooperation with Gilson, Chenu founded the Institute of Medieval Studies in Ottawa (which later moved to Montreal).

Following his exile from the Saulchoir (the result of the first of several skirmishes with Roman authorities), Chenu moved to Paris where he was invited to teach at the Sorbonne (1944 to 1951) until he eventually took a post as professor at the Institut Catholique de Paris. It is fair to say that through his teaching, friendships, and writings, Chenu was known to and in dialogue with the world's major medievalists and that he shaped many key questions in medieval studies through his unusual competence in three distinct specialties: the knowledge of the texts of St. Thomas, a solid professional grasp of Christian theology, and a formidable understanding of the historical, social, and cultural contexts out of which Aquinas's writings emerged.

Chenu had a long influence and made a deep impression upon his students. Among those who knew him and studied with him were such well-known figures as Yves Congar, Pierre-André Liégé, Edward Schillebeeckx, and later Gustavo Gutierrez—and hundreds of others who, like these, became important thinkers and writers in the Church. Chenu also was passionately involved in movements of popular catechesis and the evangelization of the working class. One of his most notable books was *The Theology of Work.*[2] Cardinal Joseph Cardijn, the founder of the Young Christian Worker movement (and of similar apostolic lay groups), remembered Chenu in the 1940s teaching his leadership teams: "Human beings cannot live outside communities; so building vibrant communities is their most fundamental apostolate. People must learn that the profound significance of human work is that it can realize God's plan for the world within our social experience."[3]

Chenu was a man of immense good humor, even in the worst of times. In the mid '50s, he gave a talk at a French regional seminary where the rector was a bit fearful that his influence on the faculty and students might be dangerous. He began his presentation with these autobiographical remarks:

"People think there are two Chenus. One is an old medievalist (with a certain reputation, perhaps) who is all taken up in reading ancient

---

[2] M. D. Chenu, *The Theology of Work*, trans. Lilian Soiron (Chicago: Regnery, 1963).

[3] J. Cardijn, "Théologie du travail, théologie pour l'homme" in *L'hommage différé au Père Chenu* (Paris: Cerf, 1990) 19.

manuscripts; he is erudite, but stuck inside a Christianity that's centuries old and inside an old tradition that absorbs him even at present. But then there is also another Chenu—young, spry, all mixed up in contemporary issues, eager to get involved in the most sensitive pastoral problems of the world and of the Church—and because of that, suspect in the eyes of some and (who knows?) a bad choice for a talk at a seminary. You wonder which one of these two persons came today? Let me tell you the truth: There is only one Chenu—a person happy to bring to you tonight what is dearest to his heart: a conversation about the mutual engagement between the patient and scholarly pursuit of theology and the apostolic impatience of the Gospel."[4]

Those words of Chenu are a good preparation for the pages that follow. You will see that Chenu would never tolerate the idea of Aquinas as an ivory tower theologian working in isolation from the burning questions of the people around him. You will also discover Chenu the storyteller who opens each chapter like a conversation, with an anecdote about the circumstances of St. Thomas's life and work. All of St. Thomas's writings were shaped by pressing academic, social, and pastoral concerns. Chenu allows us to see how apt St. Thomas's vision and views still are for many contemporary problems in the world and the Church, even though (as Thomas O'Meara puts it) this is "not to imply that [Aquinas] knew about galaxies or viruses."[5] A major feature of this book is Chenu's selection of texts from the different writings of Aquinas that complete each chapter. The reader gets a feeling for the multiple styles of Aquinas who, after all, was not just the author of the *Summa Theologiae*, but of a great array of commentaries, sermons, and poems, as well as of scholastic exercises.

One last point must be made, I think, among the many that cannot be included here because of the brief nature of this introduction. St. Thomas was a theologian. To treat him as a philosopher and to attempt to distill a Thomistic philosophy from his writings through the use of interesting texts taken out of their theological context is a mistake. As Walter Principe wrote, "Divorced from its living theological context, such a desiccated body of doctrines loses the force and vitality of Aquinas's thought and is at least partly responsible for the current

[4] M. D. Chenu, "Regard sur cinquante ans de vie religieuse" in *L'hommage différé*, op. cit., 259.

[5] Thomas F. O'Meara, *Thomas Aquinas: Theologian* (Notre Dame, Ind.: University of Notre Dame Press, 1997) ix.

neglect of his teaching in many quarters."[6] Since many of those most interested in Aquinas these days are philosophers (following the lead of Alasdair MacIntyre, Eleonore Stump, and others), Chenu's contextualizing of Aquinas's major themes will offer them precisely the kind of understanding whose absence Principe so lamented.

Ultimately St. Thomas saw theology as having an eminently practical goal. Christian revelation is historical: God changed the whole of human history through the incarnation. Christian perfection is not about escaping from the world, but about becoming agents of its transformation. The point of the Church is not maintenance of creeds and formulas of faith, but mission that will engage the whole of society. Even eschatology—the study of our ultimate human destiny—is linked to human history and has to be concerned about our human predicament in a world that continues to change dramatically. All this is clear in the following pages and a valid theological message for the present.

Chenu was a vivid personality and a charming and fluent speaker. The French text of this book, *St. Thomas d'Aquin et la théologie*, is marked by the spontaneity and pedagogical brilliance of its author. That very fact made it difficult to translate, since so many of his sentences seem interminable in the original edition. I have had the providential assistance of Myriam Frebet, O.P., in creating the English text; her help has spared me making a number of mistakes of interpretation and nuance in translating. I happily thank Fr. Thomas O'Meara who encouraged me to undertake this translation. Finally, I am pleased to say that this was a work of love and gratitude for the life of Père Chenu whom I had the privilege to know. May his profound, creative, and contemplative spirit reach out through these pages to you who take up his book and read.

Paul J. Philibert, O.P.
Aquinas Institute of Theology
St. Louis, Missouri

---

[6] Walter Principe, "St. Thomas Aquinas" in Richard P. McBrien, ed., *The Harper-Collins Encyclopedia of Catholicism* (San Francisco: HarperCollins, 1995) 84–85.

1: The Friar Preacher

At the beginning of May 1244: "Brother John of Teutonia, Master of the Order of Preachers and a man of great repute in the world of that time, spirited Brother Thomas Aquinas away from Naples, taking him out of the city where he had come to enter the order and putting him on the road for Paris. When Thomas got to Tuscany near the imperial fortress called Aquapendente (where the Emperor Frederick was then residing), Thomas's blood brother Raynald, a person of uncommon honesty and a familiar held in great favor by the prince (even though Raynald would later be put to death by him), was just then to be found at the court. As soon as Raynald heard about the approach of his younger brother, apparently without Frederick's knowledge but with the cooperation of Pierre de la Vigne, he kidnapped Thomas and took him away from the Dominican Master John. Raynald then forced Thomas on horseback and led him under strong escort into Campania, to one of the castles of his family known as San Giovanni."[1]

That is how the historian Tolomeo of Lucca—providing details of time, place, and personalities—describes the kidnapping of the young Thomas Aquinas by his family, who were opposed to his entrance into the Order of Friars Preachers. All this happened in 1244.

Thomas, then nineteen years old, was the son of Count Landolf, the Lord of Aquino, a small city about thirty kilometers from Naples. Thomas had just finished his five years of studies at the University of Naples and had taken the habit of a new religious order founded thirty years before and already in full blossom, especially in university towns. His decision had caused a sensation among the young people of Naples as well as in his family. His father, Landolf, who had died just a few months earlier, and his mother, Theodora, were completely

[1] Tolomeo of Lucca, *Historia ecclesiastica* (Roma: Muratori), col. 1152.

The narthex of the 12th cent. Church of Saint-Philibert in Tournus, France: verge opening unto the south aisle of the church; view from the lateral entrance of the church.

opposed to his vocation which ruined their hopes for him and conflicted with their worldview. Hardly had she learned the news, when Theodora dashed off to Naples, arriving too late to catch her son who was already on the road to Paris. Says the chronicler: "She sent a messenger right off to her elder sons who were at the court of the emperor at Aquapendente to ask them to kidnap Thomas, whom the Friars Preachers had robed in the habit of the order and had helped to flee from the kingdom of Naples."

Carrying out their mother's order with filial affection, Theodora's sons explained to the emperor the mission they had been asked to perform, and with his consent they sent out scouts to scour the roads and highways, according to Tolomeo.

There is no need to romanticize the details of this kidnapping. This was a time when fraternal affection could easily coexist with brute force. We should probably accept as well the attempt at feminine seduction reported by this chronicler eager for edifying material. The whole thing was undertaken within the context of the family. After a pause at Mont San Giovanni, Thomas was led off to Roccasecca, a fortified city that was the habitual residence of the Aquinas family. This was not imprisonment exactly, but rather a forced residence which would last more than a year without breaking the will of the Dominican novice who endured the affectionate constraints of his family and friends. In June or July 1245, having finally regained his freedom, Thomas went back to Naples, reentered religious life, and then took the road for Paris once again.

CHURCH AND SOCIETY

It in no way diminishes the value of this edifying story or ruins its naive expressiveness if we insist upon the sociological dimensions of the contemporary movements in which it occurs. This story offers profoundly significant indications about the kind of evolution taking place within Christianity, reaching well beyond the tale of a vocation that was violently opposed by a powerful family.

Young Thomas, third son of a small feudal lord, had been born at the fortress of Roccasecca near Aquino at the beginning of 1225 or at the end of 1224. At this time, Honorius III (1216–27) was gracefully continuing both in the church and in the world the prestigious leadership of Innocent III. Frederick II (1215–50) governed the Holy Roman Empire, from Germany to Sicily, during a period of calm relations with the papacy since the Peace of San Germano (1230). In

Thomas as the prisoner of his family. From a 19th cent. copy of a fresco in the Dominican church of Maestricht (14th cent.).

France Louis IX as still a child had begun his long reign at the very moment that the dramatic crusade against Raymond VI of Toulouse and the Albigensians turned to the benefit of the Capetian royalty.

The Muslims, still strong in Spain in the kingdom of Grenada despite the victory of the crusaders at Las Navas (1212), continued their siege of the Christian world. The fragile condition of the Latin Kingdom of Jerusalem only made the danger of Islam more obvious. Further away, pressures on Europe from the Cuman Tartars indicated the force and vitality of the Asian continent. Christianity, which had assimilated itself to the geographical and cultural influences of the Roman Empire, had once imagined that it had redeemed humanity and established the City of God on earth. But now it had to face up to

3

the fact that its faith had only touched part of humanity and that the cosmos possessed immense resources untamed by the Church.

Landolf of Aquino had been completely at home in this small feudal universe with its local rivalries and mediocre political games. He played his part in these games, hoping to place one of his sons at the head of the neighboring abbey of Monte Cassino within the confines of the Papal States and the kingdom of Naples. The abbot, a true feudal lord, had great prestige in a society where religion was able to sacralize political power. The young Thomas had been presented there as an oblate in 1230. Although this initiative of the Aquinas family was self-interested, it did not negate the fervor of the young man. However, Frederick II's invasion of Italy, following the renewal of hostilities between the papacy and the empire, cornered the Counts of Aquino, which then forced Thomas to leave the Benedictine abbey (1235). It was at that time that he had been sent to Naples to begin there, in the Faculty of Arts, a university life that only his death would interrupt.

So his pious parents objected not to a religious vocation as such, but to his entry into the Friars Preachers. These new religious came to Naples in 1231 and exercised there (as everywhere they went—so did the Friars Minor) a strong attraction among the younger generation just as they provoked a defiant opposition among their elders. "These two Orders," say the Norman Annals, "because of the novelty of their lifestyle were received with a joyful enthusiasm wherever they began to preach the word of God. The unusual quality of their life attracted to them elite personalities among the young and the cultured at the very moment that they were about to cover the face of the earth."

While the old monastic foundations lived off of their reputation of being helpful and important in the service of the Christian establishment and were economically and politically powerful in a feudal regime where they had found both institutional and spiritual privileges; new groups had arisen in many places during the preceding forty years seeking evangelical poverty, breaking with the money and the perspectives of the aristocracy, and preaching outside the feudal fortresses and monasteries so as to bring the word of God to simple people. Ordinary people thus became conscious that their past servitude was over and that great opportunities lay ahead of them. Innocent III, from a feudal background but also possessing deep apostolic lucidity, had sympathized with and favored the movement against the opposition of bishops in his entourage. Friars Preachers and Friars

L'Art Cistercien, *plate 24; the Cistercian abbey at Sénanque in southwestern France, 12ᵗʰ cent.*

Minor, the prototypes of the genre, had enjoyed his vigorous support in this surprising change of scene.

For three centuries, the Church had taken credit for the enormous effort of organizing society against the forces of chaos linked to the barbarian invasions; this effort led to the creation of the feudal system. This system provided a soul for the economy, and within it the monastery was the religious counterpart of the feudal castle. Then more recently Cîteaux, although renouncing feudal benefices, had renewed its alliance with the secular. It had sacramentalized the oath that sealed the links that held this society together and that faithfully upheld the evangelical virtues of justice and charity. It blessed the weapons of the knight so that they would be applied exclusively "in the service of widows, orphans, and the servants of God against the cruelty of the barbarians." Thus chivalry became an institution for peace: Roland and Le Cid, without being perfect Christian heroes, still represented the spirit of this religious sensibility in the midst of the brutality of this bellicose age.

With respect to economic life, chivalry had constructed from the resources of the institution of tithing a social security system that was a structure for relief assistance in the face of the frequent calamities of the age and that addressed in an almost juridical way the chronic imbalance in the distribution of goods. Hospitality, turning an evangelical counsel into a social custom, extended to daily needs in the community, to travelers, to accident victims, and to Catholic charity. The schools, created by monasteries and churches and supported both intellectually and financially by the clergy, naturally found themselves governed by ecclesiastical jurisdiction with respect to both their programs and their finances. In sum, the Church had become the buttress and the guarantee for a society in which the Church itself was the primary beneficiary. This made for a strong but strange kind of Christianity.

Three centuries of success gave these arrangements the appearance of unchangeable truth. No surprise, then, that the ecclesiastical establishment was less than thrilled at the initiatives that threatened the taken-for-granted social order. Both bishops and feudal lords were inconvenienced in parallel ways. They were upset at the disruption of tradition, and their consequent economic loss deepened their already spontaneous moral resistance. Content with the organized charity over which they held the controls, they were mostly disinterested in the developing evolution of social conditions for craftsmen and peasants.

Prizing the loyalty and the religious character of the feudal oath, they were not in favor of charters of enfranchisement which came about through violent protest. Since they saw serfdom as an honorable and permanent human condition for some, they were unable to recognize in the amelioration of the social conditions of workers any application of their own spiritual values or of the gospel's principles. Likewise, they failed to grasp at the political level the significance of the development of communes, which many bishops considered simply as the outcome of unhealthy restlessness. "The great majority of bishops remained indifferent or hostile to this movement that desired to get rid of arbitrary feudal power, itself the product of a pagan selfishness" (A. Fliche). So while they continued to preach their gospel of justice and charity, their temporal interests blinded them to the social transformations that were needed. Those among them who tried to extirpate abuses and vice within the system were witnesses to the hopeless inefficacy of a purely moralistic reform movement. In the end, they lacked any understanding of the "new humanity" about to appear.

During this transition from fief to commune, the new movement's leaders had progressively acquired the autonomy to take initiatives, a feeling of personal responsibility, a taste for change, and the creativity that flowed into the mastery of the unforeseen problems of a world newly open to innovation. The urban schools, filled with youth from these new sectors of society, were linked to the life of the communes and to the guilds in their success as well as in their impatience; it was there that the social evolution could be most clearly recognized. Thomas Aquinas's birth had located him within a high feudal dynasty and his family traditions had destined him for one of the most powerful abbeys. (He had even passed his youth at Monte Cassino.) Yet, by his determined insistence, he entered into a Dominican vocation and onto a path that would lead him to the most volatile and most representative of the urban schools at the heart of this new society, the University of Paris.

THE GOSPEL AT THE HEART OF SOCIAL CHANGE

Set apart from the world yet still present to it—that is the paradox of the gospel. Within the new movement, this same paradox was as captivating and astonishing as in the Gospels themselves: poverty even more than asceticism was the effective symbol of their power. Thomas Aquinas's refusal of Monte Cassino is the exact parallel to Francis of Assisi's gesture of renunciation, even down to the dramatic details of their different episodes. But not only individuals can live in poverty, institutions can as well. (Some individuals, of course, also lived in poverty even within a rich Church.) But the friars faced day after day the need to beg for their daily bread, renouncing the economic stability and social power which had been the support of their elders and the source of the monastery's influence. The friars could not have been clearer about their choice.

They also guarded themselves against the danger of riches coming from the vitality of the new social order, even while they counted on it to generate a Christianity that would provide for its new apostles. In this way, mendicant poverty became both the economic structure for itinerant preachers who traveled far and wide as well as the spirit of a community of "brothers" who joyously threw themselves upon the devices of divine Providence. No more of majestic monastic buildings as immovable as fortified castles! The friars needed poor, temporary residences found in the student neighborhoods near to the city folk. Only people who identified with these new apostles and their fraternal spirit would undertake to house, feed, and support them.

The structure of government which the Friars Preachers adopted, both instinctively and consciously, is the juridical expression of their gospel fraternity. At every level, authority is exercised not by persons appointed from on high, but through elections at every echelon of Dominican life in a rotation of responsibilities that assures to the community its irreplaceable autonomy and, through its chosen representatives, the inspiration and the stability of self-government. No longer does the religious obey one person in an order marked by paternalistic warmth but also by the subjectivism of the superior; rather the friar obeys the function within which the common good is objectified, conceived and institutionalized through the whole brotherhood of the order.

From the first, the Preachers did away with the title "abbot" and elected a "prior." The requirements of community government are not the wishes of a prince (however pious they might be), but rather the expression of the objective rational discernment of a community's common consent. Even in its organizational principles, the Dominican Order, by its gospel inspiration, is the source and guide for a spirituality and soon (thanks to Thomas Aquinas) for a theology of society that will turn away from arbitrary authority of every stripe.

These details show the significance of the step taken by Brother Thomas and suggest how it will shape both his religious life and his doctrinal perspective. Here is clearly seen the great importance of mendicant poverty and its influence on his life. It is a "foolish" gospel inspiration that makes no sense at all to "wise" people. Its role in the period's social evolution in no way diminishes its mystical motivation; to the contrary, mendicant poverty is an incarnation of the religious spirit of the order. To vow "mendicancy" in the thirteenth century was to refuse the feudal system of the Church both institutionally and economically, including benefices and the collection of tithes, even when they were destined for apostolic and charitable purposes. It was also to dislodge the free proclamation of the word of God from the heavy apparatus of feudalism.

Neither Francis nor Dominic ever explicitly dreamed of taking an option for or against the economic order as such. Beyond that, the

Church had neither the grace nor the competence to create, elaborate, or oppose a technical system to control earthly wealth. The mendicants renounced feudalism in the same way that liberation movements have separated themselves from capitalism, by gospel inspiration, not by ideological persuasion.* The return to the gospel brings about a break with debilitating institutional structures as well as with inappropriate personal behavior.

In this way, poverty is seen as the effective symbol of a return to gospel principles as well as the first step in moving toward a revival of pure gospel living according to its original and literal demands. The first, really the *only* rule chosen by St. Francis was a few verses of the gospel, not a new religious program comparable with the *Rule of St. Augustine* or the *Rule of St. Benedict*. "Don't talk to me about any other form of life than that which the Lord has himself mercifully shown and given to me" *(Legenda Antiqua)*. This gospel that comes from Christ has to be held on to in its pristine force, without glosses or commentaries that can easily dissolve the demanding claim of its vision.

Likewise for the Friars Preachers, their life emerges from the rediscovery of the gospel's Good News linked to their confidence in a lifestyle of poverty without regard for traditional means of gaining power or influence. Dominic, their founder, is called by his successor and biographer *vir evangelicus*—man of the gospel.[2] Thomas Aquinas's attraction to the friars (despite the strong opposition of his family) and the unusual esteem which the Franciscans and Dominicans immediately received from the generation of young adults testify to this revival of the word of God in the Church.

Should we miss the shock that this evangelical revival caused not only for individuals but also for institutions, the determined opposition that the Preachers and the Friars Minor received would make us aware of it. Early on Thomas used his lucid genius to debate those who sought to deny the "new apostles" not this or that canonical privilege, but their very right to exist. This gave him the occasion to make explicit the deep reasons for his vocation and to define the religious and apostolic nature of the mendicants.

* In Chenu's original, he speaks of the "Mission de France" rather than of liberation movements.

[2] Jordan of Saxony, *Libellus on the Beginnings of the Order of Preachers*, in *Monumenta Ordinis Praedicatorum Historica*, ed. H. C. Scheeben (Roma: MOPH, 1935), vol. 16, 75.

William of Saint-Amour, a Master of the University of Paris, supported by several bishops, undertook during these years to critique not only the canonical status but also the doctrinal foundation of what he would call a *new gospel* created by these pseudo-prophets of the new age. His pamphlet, *De periculis novissimorum temporum* ("On the Dangers of these Last Days"), reached five editions. His complaints were these: these religious were involved in the world, when by their religious state they should be separated from the world; their poverty was endangering the good order of society and private property; they were exercising apostolic ministries for which they had no mandate; and they were teaching, when they ought to maintain a humble silence. Beyond his own personal animosity, his attack represented the reactionary conservatism of many others. Ultimately the gospel itself was being put to the test by these promoters of a new Christianity.

Public opinion became passionately engaged in the matter, as one can see in reading Rutebeuf or Jean de Meung or even the *Roman de Renart*. At the beginning of the academic year 1255, the protection of the king's archers was needed for the opening days of courses at the Dominican priory of Saint-Jacques because the quarrel had become so divisive. Therefore Thomas Aquinas would have to defend the spirit, the institutions, and the functions of the two orders twice: in 1256 along with St. Bonaventure the Franciscan and again in 1270 alone. His replies to the treatises and pamphlets of his adversaries—"men both perverse and shrewd," he called them—are the theological articulation of his initial choice for the Friars Preachers at the University of Naples. Even before his *Summa Theologiae* had expressed his thoughts about the "states of life" with serenity and organically linked them to his theological work (II–II, 183–9) in a treatise for which St. Thomas would remain considered for centuries the master of the spiritual life, the Apostolic See would side with this mendicant catechetical movement not only by confirming the new orders, but also by supporting their teaching. Condemned, William of Saint-Amour was forced to leave the University of Paris in 1256.

The evangelical movement fostered not only a new institution, but similar to the institution, a new doctrinal vision: "a new way of thinking, of reasoning, and of articulating the meaning of religion" (Daniel-Rops). Thomas the theologian is the son of Dominic the preacher. And the Preachers are unthinkable without St. Thomas.

Set apart from the world, yet still present to it: this is the paradox of the Christian in the world. God's presence to the whole of human reality, carnal as well as spiritual, impacts not only the level of actions, both individual and collective; the divine presence extends as well, following the logic of the incarnation and of the Spirit, to the exercise of human reasoning. These evangelical thinkers are deeply involved in the civilization of their time and concern themselves with all kinds of problems: from that of the cities of Lombardy fighting to get their charters of freedom with the help of the mendicants, to that of sharing the exhilarating discovery of Greek thought with the faithful— leading to its exploitation and promotion in their theology.

Grace thus allows nature to be free to be itself, and leads it on to its perfection in both communities and individuals, in both action and contemplation. The gospel paradox again is made clear by this formula of Thomas. Faith makes reason free to be itself both in its own proper order of reasoning as well as in the understanding of faith. Theology is "evangelical" when it confers on reason, on its methods, and its objects their proper value: its goal is to guarantee the transcendence of the Word of God with the freedom of faith. Further, "a philosophy becomes more Christian by becoming more truly philosophy" (E. Gilson).[3] By being more truly civilization in the human context, civilization qualifies as being more Christian. In the realm of the gospel, "separation" is only for the sake of "presence." The evangelical vocation of Brother Thomas Aquinas is the source of the development of his theology.

TEXTS

The Rule of Saint Francis

In the name of the Lord: here begins the life of the Friars Minor.

The Rule and the life of the Friars Minor consist in observing the holy gospel of our Lord Jesus Christ, in living in obedience, and in having nothing that belongs to oneself . . .

To those who will come to find our brothers, seeking to share their life . . . , say to them this word of the holy gospel: let them sell

---

[3] Étienne Gilson, *L'esprit de la philosophie médiévale* (Paris, 1932) vol. 1, 187.

everything that they possess and distribute it to the poor. Then we will give them the habit of a novice, namely: two tunics without a capuce, the cord, britches, and a cape that reaches down to the belt.

. . . The brothers should not own anything, neither a house, land, nor anything else. Like pilgrims and strangers in this world (1 Pet. 2:11), serving the Lord in poverty and humility, they will go out to seek alms with confidence and without shame, for the Lord made himself poor in this world.

Such is the grandeur of this wonderful poverty, my very dear brothers, that it has made you heirs and kings in the kingdom of heaven, poor in earthly goods, but lifted up in virtue. Let poverty be your share—as it leads you into the land of the living. Dearly beloved, commit yourselves totally to poverty, and for the name of our Lord Jesus Christ refuse forever to have anything else under the sun.

Wherever the brothers are or they meet together, make sure that they serve one another. Let them make their needs known one to the other in all confidence; for if a mother nourishes and cherishes her son born according to the flesh, with even more affection should each of us love and nourish our brother according to the Spirit!

Regula secunda: I, 2, 6.

Letter of Recommendation for the Preachers

Honorius, bishop and servant of the servants of God, to his venerable brothers—archbishops and bishops—and to his dear sons who are prelates of all the churches to which this proclamation shall reach: health and apostolic benediction.

If it is true that to receive a prophet because he is a prophet, is to merit the reward of a prophet (Matt 10:41), then we rightly commend to you all these men consecrated to preaching who are more than necessary to the life of the Holy Church, since they provide for it the nourishment of the Word of God. Thus you will earn an incomparable reward in helping them.

This is why we have very willingly taken them under our sponsorship and so we recommend to you our dear sons, the Preachers, who by their profession of poverty and of the regular life are completely dedicated to the proclamation of God's Word. We both ask you and exhort you by this order given by apostolic decree to receive them immediately with charity when they arrive in your region of the world to carry out the ministry of preaching to which they have been deputed; and to eagerly inform the people in your charge so that they will accept with devotion from their mouth the seed of the Word of God. Assist them generously in all their needs, out of consideration for God and for ourselves . . .

Apply yourselves to helping them so earnestly that, with your cooperation, they will happily complete the course of ministry that has been confided to them and obtain the desired outcome of their work and their goal, which is the salvation of souls.

Given at the Lateran, the second day of the Nones of February, in the fifteenth year of our pontificate.

2: Master in Sacred Theology

Finally free, Thomas started back on the road for Paris—toward the University of Paris. The young Neapolitan novice was being sent into this great city precisely so that he could undertake his doctrinal training in the schools of Paris—more famous than any other—in contrast to the educational habits of the monastic tradition.

Setting up a priory in the middle of the city, whether in Naples or Paris, was a significant choice. This geographical shift was the institutional expression of a spiritual shift as well. The religious house built right in the city became for both the Preachers and the Friars Minor—through the city's access to vocation recruitment, clientele for pastoral work, new collective structures, and new flexibility in both law and apostolates—the natural environment where all the social, cultural, and spiritual innovations were being expressed and making their impact. Monastic observance thus moved off of solitary mountaintops and out of hidden valleys into the center of the big cities.

This is more than symbolic. In these same cities, the schools are the places where the new awareness and the new initiatives are being dreamed up. Populated with the new generation, the schools express through their intellectual life and their educational programs the same aspirations for social life and for the organization of the city that are being expressed by the corporations and the municipal courts. The schools of Paris could not have been more different from the monastic schools. Monastery schools were tied to an immovable corps of teachers, governed by the paternalism of the abbot, and representative of the spirit of feudalism, where monasticism had found its social support. On the contrary, the schools of Paris were organized according to free association and governed by an elective system that chose both faculty and administration.

Painting of Thomas Aquinas by Justus le Gand,
Bibliothèque Nationale de France.

We need to be careful in referring to the decline of monastic studies in the thirteenth century, however. Quite a number of masterpieces were produced—and would continue to be produced—which could outclass some of the products of the schools. But even the most successful personal or local achievements of the monasteries could not hide the great institutional shift that took place in the course of the century because of social and cultural change. A new class of people came to the schools at Paris, Bologna, Oxford, and Cologne. From the first they were a crowd that quickly overflowed the cathedral cloisters and therefore they created a neighborhood for themselves where they could be in charge—even in the streets (where turbulence reigned). These were the students of Abelard, not those of Anselm.

The "university" of studies, within which these schools grouped themselves spontaneously, is one of the institutions of the new city, fashioned after the pattern of the guilds of craftsmen. The same human intuition inspires both the liberal arts and the mechanical arts. Masters and students compose a veritable intellectual "internationale," divided into four "nations": French, English (including England and Germany), Picard (the Netherlands), and Norman.

This university constituted a collective juridical entity with the competence to solve its own problems, and thus was raised to an official rank within the city. It gained, even by means going on strike, the right to organize its own life according to its free choice. It had its own police force as well. All this required, however, that it still respect the rights of the larger collective, the city. Focused directly upon intellectual and cultural values, the university easily moved beyond the context of the city to offer its advice on the life of politics. It willingly offered its judgment on such issues out of its universal concern for human dignity.

Both masters and students enjoyed a "state" that was entitled not only to its "rights and freedoms," but also benefited from a moral and soon a political prestige, to the advantage or the detriment of higher learning. (The aristocratic academies of the Renaissance will lose this kind of insertion of intellectuals and theologians into the political life of the society.)

When St. Bernard in a famous rude remark severely berated the students in Paris, this was not just the expression of his moral rigorism condemning the customary dissoluteness of youth, but the reaction of a religious ideal scandalized by a complete compromise with the world. In his view, the university, by its support of the new developments, profaned the old spiritual culture. In fact, Cîteaux, which gave a magnificent luster to monastic life, had clearly broken away from this new world, building its abbeys far from the cities, sending its monks back to doing manual labor, reducing study to spiritual reading, and condemning dialectic and the other profane studies. The true school for them was the "school of divine service," according to the perfect definition that St. Benedict had given for the monastery, thus shaping the content and the structures of the monastic school where Christ is the Master.

The success of the urban schools, competitive in spirituality even more than in pedagogy, turned the comparison with the monastic school into an antinomy: the monk should avoid the urban schools. Indeed monks should glory in the fact that they didn't roam from city to city like Abelard in pursuit of science and culture seeking famous "chairs" of teaching. Rupert, the abbot of Deutz (1120), a tough adversary of the schools of Laon (one of the first free communes), expressed his faithful adherence to the Rule of St. Benedict in his rejection of these rich "merchants of science" who along with their itinerant clientele had treated him like a poor ignoramus. Pierre de Celle, the abbot of Saint Remy in Reims (1162–80), a man of refined personal culture, in a letter to his friend John of Salisbury, headmaster of the schools of Chartres, claimed absolute value for the true school where the student doesn't pay his master, where no one is distracted by vain curiosity, where students do not give themselves over to discussion, where every question is predetermined and every reason understood—the blessed school of Christ, far from the disappointing seductions of Paris.

THE UNIVERSITY OF PARIS

Brother Thomas was sent to these "seductive and disappointing" schools in Paris not by some casual choice for a precocious young student, but by a logical decision on the part of the Preachers, whose founder Dominic had sent his very first group to take courses at the urban school of Toulouse (1215). The first group of preaching friars in Paris had been welcomed, housed, and immediately accredited by the masters of the University of Paris (1221).

Somewhere around 1200, Paris had become the school of schools. From the last third of the twelfth century on, it became the counselor of princes and prelates. In 1169, Henry II of England had proposed to submit his dispute with Thomas Beckett to the judgment of the assembled Masters of Paris. Paris was, in the phrase of the pope, the oven where the intellectual bread of the Latin world was baked. Elsewhere they suckled babies; here they fed robust appetites. The Masters of Arts (Letters and Sciences), in the context of speaking about their colleague Thomas Aquinas, will call it "the noblest city for the life of the spirit" at a moment when for the first time in human history the life of the spirit was expressed in a collective organism where tradition and creativity were linked together. This was the University.

During the second half of the thirteenth century, a decentralization became necessary. But the effects of this change had not yet disturbed the spiritual and institutional primacy of the French university, at least not in philosophy and theology, when Thomas was teaching there. Paris was the intellectual center of Christianity because of its accumulated resources, its teaching personnel, its international recruitment, its professional and pedagogical organization, its scholarly traditions, its technical superiority, its spirit of curiosity, and its creative inspiration. It was the domain *par excellence* of high culture. "The city of philosophers," Albert the Great called it—the new Athens. It was no coincidence for Thomas to be sent to Paris to make a career there. The rules of his order, the directives of the Church, and the social movements of the times all contributed to his ending up there. St. Thomas's spiritual and institutional development is unthinkable out-

Painting of Saint Albert the Great by Thomas of Modena, 1352.

side of Paris. Naples, Viterbo, and Rome are merely episodes in his intellectual development and in his career. Paris is his natural habitat.

Thomas found at Paris not only a milieu, but within this milieu a man who in his thought had already opened a pathway and in his works already cleared the landscape—Albert of Cologne. At the time of their first meeting in 1245, Albert already enjoyed an extensive prestige that was also controversial, even among his friars. Albert in no way hid his purpose: he proposed to make Greek science and reason, personified by the recently discovered Aristotle, understandable to the medieval Latin world. He threw himself into this actively, almost feverishly. Between 1240 and 1248, hurried on by some, blamed by others, Albert had produced within the schools of Paris (where it was still officially forbidden to teach Aristotle) five commentaries on Aristotle's works of natural philosophy, the *Physics* at the top of the list, and on his other works, including the *Treatise on the Soul*.

Albert's teaching, if not his publications, had created a sensation, to the point that Albert is soon cited (to the scandal of Roger Bacon) as on the same level as the traditional authorities. His care to present himself as a simple interpreter, along with his vivid replies to his detractors, underlined the courage of his work. He was courageous in insisting on the methodology that justifies the independence of research within the context of each discipline: "In treating faith and morals, we must trust St. Augustine more than the philosophers, should there be a disagreement. But if we treat of medicine, I place myself in the hands of Galen and Hippocrates; and if we treat of the nature of things, I turn to Aristotle or to some other expert in this area of study." A reflection at the beginning of his commentary on the *Analytics* shows how his spirit opened itself to multiple perspectives on intelligibility and progress: "The sciences are not yet all established, and there remain a good number yet to be discovered." Albert was the first person in the history of western thought "to define the role of the sciences within Christianity" (F. Van Steenberghen).[1]

The chroniclers of the time have recorded the fond and trusting mutual understanding that existed between Master Albert and his disciple, first at Paris from 1245 to 1248, then at Cologne from 1248 to 1252, where St. Thomas wrote an account *(reportatio)* of the questions of his professor on the *Ethics* of Aristotle. The fond relationship

---

[1] Cf. F. van Steenberghen, *Siger de Brabant d'après ses oeuvres inédites,* vol. 2 of *Siger de Brabant dans l'histoire de l'aristotélisme* (Louvain, 1942) 468–79.

between the two men would be lasting: we need only remember how Albert devotedly returned to Paris in 1277 in order to defend the reputation and the doctrinal works of St. Thomas after his condemnation.

There were nonetheless some differences on doctrinal positions between the master and his disciple, whether in their conclusions or their overall perspective. Albert's key concern was to coordinate with Aristotelian experimentalism a Platonic spirituality rooted in his own temperament and in his own philosophical and theological sensibilities that were quite different from Thomas's. So it is difficult to measure Albert's exact influence upon the construction of Thomist doctrine. But on a spiritual level, there was profound understanding between them, as can be seen by the fate of their common theological enterprise.

In any case, Albert's influence in establishing the program of studies for the first Preachers put in place a regime of philosophical work and a scientific spirit that defined the natural role of the order within both the university movement and the cultural developments of their time. From the start of his teaching career, Thomas Aquinas is carried along by the grace of the Order of Preachers, which reciprocally recognized in his doctrine its own evangelical spirit.

FAITH AND THEOLOGY

Back in Paris in 1252, Thomas taught in a climate that was both tense and warmly supportive, as events allow us to understand. From 1256 on, given the title of Master prematurely on the insistence of Pope Alexander IV (who grandly eulogized his work), Thomas took charge of one of the two schools of the priory and university college of Saint-Jacques.

This helps us situate the nature of his work and to foresee the literary genre in which he will express his own spiritual vision. He will write not a confidential revelation of his religious experience nor a testimony of his "confessions" in the style of Augustine, nor with the affective soulfulness of a mystic. Rather he will compose teachings with precise technical formulas for his specialized audience, their dialogical structure preserved in the text; his writings will also convey the reflective distance that characterizes the best of pedagogy. Theology is a bit detached from pastoral life. One runs a significant risk in doing theology this way, but it accords with the nature of theological investigation and follows the guidance of the Spirit's inspiration.

Genius and holiness—or more simply faith—will dominate his profession as a theologian, but the profession itself will remain a normal expression of academic work. The medieval university will refine and perfect its expression. Within this highly structured technical ambiance, Thomas's writings will become masterpieces. We have only to think of a chapter of Thomas's *Contra Gentiles* or a passage of Bonaventure's *Itinerarium mentis* to remind ourselves that the highest and purest spiritual insights can be at home within this literary context.

Such courses (or lectures, as the English still call them) are clearly a far cry from the old-fashioned spiritual conference of the abbot to his monks. The key difference between these two forms of teaching, however, is due not so much to a different technical approach as to a different inspiration. Since the twelfth century, Master (*magister*) was the title for the head of the bands of itinerant preachers—for example, Robert d'Arbrissel, Norbert of Prémontré, and Dominic himself. These evangelists refused the title *abbot* or lord (*Dom*) that went along with temporal powers and responsibilities. The title Master refers to the entire effort of bearing witness to the Word of God, following the development of three homogeneous activities: *reading* (a text as foundation), *arguing* (a question or a problem), and *preaching*.

In fact it is difficult during these two or three first generations to tell the difference between these literary genres in works where a lecture is at the same time teaching and preaching. The responsibilities of the Master will be defined in the context of this apostolic creativity where all three functions normally arise from the profession of the theologian. The master *in sacra pagina*, as they called him, was responsible for preaching: the theology of the Word of God is only complete when the divine message has been transmitted to someone. Exegesis, dogmatic theology, and pastoral theology all go together for someone who understands the gospel, since all of them require entering into the active presence of the Word for their realization. Theology arises out of, develops, and fulfills itself in the atmosphere of this living Word received in faith. Master Thomas teaches continuously on the text of the Bible, which is the foundational text for the Faculty of Theology. His *Summa Theologiae*, despite its technical methodology, can only be understood properly as a living emanation from the *pagina sacra* (the sacred page of the Bible).

This is how theology, arising out of the gospel, came to be seen as a *science*. Neither the institutional structure of the university nor the method of a professional scholar should hide this pedagogical and spiritual continuity that exists between gospel and theology. In any case, whatever opinion one might hold about the matter, here is the

L'Art Cistercien, *plate 58;
a medieval passageway,
12th cent.*

source of Thomas's spirituality; he is a doctor of the Church *because*
he is a master in theology. He was fully conscious of this sacred quality of theology; furthermore, he is the one who set down the rules for
maintaining a theological stance. It will always be true that the practice of this high wisdom following these rules will reach beyond the
theoretical and methodological principles at hand, and will allow us
to read theology in the incandescent atmosphere of the Spirit that
gave them birth. We can only grasp Thomas's spirituality by master-
ing a devoted familiarity with the whole theological endeavor that was
his teaching as a doctor. The expositions that Thomas's reflections
and methodology produce furnish us with a solid base for our own
theological analysis.

The Word of God is heard in the context of faith. This Word can
only be received in faith. Even in human dialogue with another person, exchanging words with one another, a certain bare minimum of
trust is the fundamental condition for dialogue. Thomas borrows
from Augustine this theme of the necessity of faith for human encounter. But when God is the partner, this psychological necessity becomes doubly important because of the radical demand arising from

the very nature of the human spirit. The human mind needs to be lifted up *(elevatio)* to the level of its divine partner, whose life continues to remain totally mysterious. In this way, faith lifts up my intelligence to the mystery of this transcendent being who speaks to me. Faith is a theological virtue in the strict sense of the term, since from the start it confers on me a participation in the divine nature. Without that, how could there be dialogue?

This marvel of faith is astonishing for this reason as well: in order to undertake and achieve the dialogue, God becomes human. As a result of this disconcerting initiative, since God is going to speak to me as a human being, I am going to undertake to dialogue with God as a human—first in the Scriptures, then (and supremely so) in the incarnation, and finally in his Church which continues to be his body. My faith will not bring about a mystical transport beyond my human condition, but rather a communion at my own psychological level achieved in human words with the capacity to proclaim God in my own earthly formulations, using human grammar and expressions. In Christ, the Word of God has spoken to me in a dialogue that is consubstantial with my humanity. Certainly I should have no illusions about the frailty of what my words can say: in this context they can never be adequate to what they utter. But however strained they may be, I can be sure that they will, following their intended meaning and by the Church's assurance, authentically contain the truth of the Word of God.

Theology then will arise out of the experience of faith. Because it is implanted within my human spirit, faith will never be like something extrinsic introduced into my living organism or like a list of dead propositions in my spirit—in my "heart"—as scripture often puts it. Rather it is a force within me whose dynamic intelligence becomes a kind of appetite for its own fulfillment in the beatifying vision of God (of which it is already the first beginnings). In this encounter of object and subject—of God-as-object and me-as-subject—all the normal dynamics of psychology come into play, just as philosophers will describe them.

The object first of all is the source of understanding. However, this is an act of revelation which by the light of faith raises me to the level of God's transcendence. It is an initiation into God's mystery and God's merciful incarnation. The Living God, subsistent Truth, does not come to me as a simple mental object; rather God offers me communion as a gift of the Holy Spirit that grows through love. If I remain faithful, if my faith surrenders to this trust and to this message, God will nourish me with his presence. This mystery concerning God's action in the world, God's action upon humanity, is received in my own life—received by my intelligence, given to me to feed and nourish me.

On the other side, there is a human hunger, stimulated by this divine gift, that grows out of the endless curiosity of my spirit. Is not the search for causes the most significant and deepest act of human intelligence? And among causes, the strongest impulse is for the first of causes. My act of faith stimulates an insatiable, ardent search to discover and reach out to this first Cause, and to have "science"—absolutely trustworthy knowledge—of God and of God's economy of creation. My faith is entirely captivated by this yearning for a vision in which the incomprehensibility of the divine energies that draw me into the interior life of God can become my own. Faith is thus the real inception of the beatific vision, the foretaste of future contemplation—"the substance of goods to be hoped for, the proof of realities still invisible" (Heb 11:1).

This kind of activity cannot be some anonymous act within a collective fusion of persons with Christ for the sake of their divinization. This thrust of faith towards God takes place within an interior personal relation, as is fitting for an act of love. The divine community of human beings who live in Christ is a community of persons. It comes about through and within the experience of faith where the freedom of each one is not only the fundamental condition of encounter, but the very structure of mutual love. This radical interiority remains motivated purely by delight in the Word of God addressed to me, even though rational investigation can (and sometimes ought to) establish a motive of credibility. St. Gregory said, "Faith would lose its validity if human reason were to furnish its support."

Clearly, at the risk of dissolving the very meaning of this transcendent communion, faith has a representational content immanent within it. It is articulated in a collection of propositions or judgments constructed upon the logic of human statements—"dogmatic formulas"—which the Church, as earthly teacher and instructor of this revelation, proposes and defines. But these formulas are not the end point of faith. Beyond them, faith reaches out to the mysterious reality of God as God is. This "intentionality" of faith gives the formulas of faith their life, and through them opens the human soul to God. This is how faith is a light attuned to the divine nature.

Within this illumination, God appears as the First Truth (in the sense that metaphysical language uses for ultimate reality)—Subsistent Truth, Personal Truth. The light of faith carries an unquestionable authority and calls for spiritual obedience. This is not like a simple passive submission to a voice from the outside. When we adhere to God-as-Truth, when we then seek to understand this Truth in theology, we so act not just because God has spoken the truth, but because God knows and is the truth of ultimate reality and calls us to take part in knowing it.

Thus understood, faith and the theology of faith express the dynamics of a personal commitment of spirit to spirit; here my assent by grace is released by my will for salvation. If God were to reveal to me mathematical, physical, or historical truths, there would not be the same role for the will to play. God would not be offering his very self to me and my personal interior response would not be so engaged. Twentieth-century philosophers would say that this is a case of existential knowledge. In the language of St. Thomas we can say that the Spirit testifies within me. This is not some vague sentimental experience. The Spirit's testimony invites belief, an intimate action of a totally different kind than the objective impersonal conviction of a mathematical theorem, a law of nature, or even a philosophical demonstration (whatever the role of the intelligence in the matter may be). This clarifies the role of spirituality in theology, which is the understanding of the object of faith—the *intellectus fidei*.

It follows that by its very nature faith is pregnant with theology by reason of the spontaneous development of its own grace. Understand "theology" in its full sense and according to its fullest expression: theo-logy means understanding about God—whether this be the simple penetration of a gazing upon the divine, the expression in full adult faith of the conscious possession of its object, the organized technical knowledge of the type characteristic of human science, or the pastoral transmission of the gospel message.

It takes nothing away from theology as a science in the strict sense, to situate it within the generic meaning that the Ancients gave to the term; they emphasized theology's mystical character more than its technical methodology. St. Thomas stays faithful to Denis the Areopagite on this point, since he knows the writings of Denis, having commented upon them in his courses.

The fruitfulness of faith touches the multiple aspects of human spirituality; the light of divine faith becomes "incarnated" as it were within the human spirit. This "cogitatio" (reflective reasoning), as St. Thomas calls it following Augustine, develops along with the assent given to the Word of God (whether as intuition or through the engagement of the many aspects of intelligence—or through both at the same time) as an affective reaching out toward the understanding of what we believe. The assent of faith does not close down after making an objective act of obedience; rather, it unleashes human curiosity so that natural human intelligence and the grace of faith work in complementary fashion.

Once, at the end of a *disputatio* (debate) in the university where the legitimacy of reasoning faith was contested by the proponents of a faith understood as pure obedience, St. Thomas gave a magisterial defense of the value and necessity of the investigation of the "roots" of divine truth for a community of believers in these words: "If we resolve the problems posed by faith exclusively by means of authority, we will of course possess the truth—but in empty heads!" (*Quodlibet IV*, art. 16—Paris, 1271).

That being the case, the act of the theologian (which is both contemplative and speculative at the same time) is not only adoration, devotion, and worship (all acts belonging to the virtue of religion); rather theological work fits precisely within the rhythm of that graced life created within us by the virtues of faith, hope, and charity. The teachings of the theology professor, like the acts of the practicing Christian, find their truth and their worth within these theological virtues; otherwise, they lose their theological status. Theology, even in its most rudimentary expression, protects believers against the danger of vacuous sociological conformity, whether pedagogical or sacramental.

Fides quaerens intellectum, faith seeking understanding: this was the definition of theology proposed by St. Anselm, the great monastic theologian of the twelfth century. Now we can see the power and the implications of this formula. Theology is not eccentric, uninviting, dangerous work. It is, we might dare to say, an act signifying faith's robust health. Faith's appetite (as in the life of the body) is the clearest indication of its vibrant equilibrium. Appetite can be, of course, a nonreflective, simple physical instinct. But if I become aware of and take charge of my desires, appetite then expresses my essential vitality and warns me of my weaknesses. The appetite of faith serves this same function in the work of theology.

Are we right to speak here of health or of equilibrium? Yes, indeed. Sometimes, at certain graced moments, you can find yourself within a kind of theological euphoria that becomes even a sort of intoxication expressing the heights of communion with divine reality—with the disorienting mystery of God-as-Object. Theologians can lose their footing in the "immense sea of the divine substance"[2] (John Damascene, cited by Aquinas), because the more they commune with this Life, the more they recognize how elusive it is and how dissimilar they are to the Mystery that stretches their understanding. *Sobria ebrietas*—sober intoxication: this ancient expression of the Platonic philosophers is appropriate to the truth of what happens within theology. Now that God has become human and that we are the children of God in the earthly fellowship of his Son, the intoxication of the pagan mystics becomes true wisdom.

Nowhere in the writings of St. Thomas will you find an echo of this affective intoxication, yet a number of episodes related by his contemporaries reveal to us—beneath their hagiographic trappings—his intense contemplative concentration, which sometimes carried him away from the modest course of his material concerns or of his professional work. The following phrase of Thomas's about the work of the theologian, austere and dense as it is, should be read and weighed in the light of his experience: "In the fervor of their faith, Christians love the truth that they believe. They examine it and reflect upon it, and they embrace it while searching according to their ability for reasons for the *cogitatio* (reflective musing) and the love that are part of faith."[3]

They search for reasons because reasoning is one of the resources of the spirit for embracing the object of human desire. Within the spectrum of acts that run from the first impulsive image all the way to the highest experience of the soul's contemplation, there is an entire zone of activity that belongs to what we call reasoning—the reasoning that searches for reasons, that poses questions, that calls into question— why that way?! This questioning includes the whole field of our understanding, from the indiscrete ingenuousness of the child speaking to his mother to the methodical research of the scholar who weighs how to attain the internal essence of beings and their intelligibility. This rationality, even when it sometimes renders reality dry and dusty, does nothing to devalue the rich liveliness of other, more spontaneous assets, such as affective intuition (where sensibilities fine or

---

[2] St. John Damascene, *De fide orthodoxa,* Book 1, ch. 9 (see Migne, *Patrologia Latina,* Vol. 94, col. 835), cited in *Summa Theologiae,* I, q. 13, art. 11.

[3] *Summa Theologiae,* II–II, q. 2, art. 10.

less fine come into play). Rather, human reasoning, contrary to the nature of pure spirit, can only penetrate the meaning of its object and become master of itself when it applies itself to its characteristic function of searching for reasons.

Here is how believing theologians go about their work: following the lead of an instinctive discernment and with careful discretion, they apply all the techniques of reasoning for the sake of a perception of divine mystery. This includes the pulling apart of concepts, the multiplication of analyses and judgments, definition, division, comparison and classification, inference, middle terms, and finally deduction. I was going to say "above all, deduction," in as much as deduction can be the characteristic operation of science within which the reasoning process achieves its efficacy. The same law which makes us require an incarnation of the Word of God within human words through the course of history now obliges us to accept to the end the structure of knowledge that this incarnation implies. Theology is essentially linked to the theandric mystery of the Word of God—Word made flesh. Theology's audacious trust in the coherence of faith and reason is rooted in the mystery of the incarnation.

You cannot share this confidence in the mystery and then be afraid of an intrusion of reason within the new synthesis we mentioned. There is a famous remark of Bonaventure, the Franciscan Master of the neighboring school next to Thomas's in Paris: he said that he was more attentive to the intrusion than to the synthesis, and recalled the dream of St. Jerome who saw himself being whipped at the last judgment for having taken pleasure in reading Cicero. Bonaventure denounced the use of philosophy in theology by many, including the Friars Preachers, saying: "It is like mixing water in the pure wine of the Word of God." Thomas, taking up the terms of the miracle of Cana, replied, somewhat humorously, "It's not a case of mixing water in the wine, but of turning water into wine."

The introduction of rational propositions into the exposition of faith is not the perversion that some wish to make it out to be. A mystical theology is not created by evicting speculative theology. Sacred doctrine is unified, despite the diversity of its functions, by the unity of faith; yet the transcendence of the divine word in no way diminishes sacred doctrine's human characteristics. Theology, which is faith expressed in theological understanding, is properly and truly an aspect of the spiritual life. You don't create a theology by adding pious phrases to abstract theses withdrawn from their textual and interpretive contexts. Theology is unified by the profound unity of divine faith. Thomas Aquinas is a saint in and through his work as a theologian. His sanctity continuously engages and nourishes his occupation as a professor, exercised day and night in a university where he is completely at home.

We may have difficulty in imagining this kind of unity of faith and theology, like Thomas's own contemporaries, who were struck—some in admiration, others in shock—by this theology that gives human expression to faith. The chronicler William of Tocco described this strong reaction in a passage where the hammering repetition of the word "new" expressed the shock provoked by the teaching of the young Master: "In his course, Brother Thomas raised new problems, discovered new methods, employed new kinds of proofs; and in hearing him thus teach a new doctrine, with new arguments, you could not doubt that God, through the radiance of this new light and by the novelty of his inspiration, had given him a new doctrine to teach by both speaking and writing." Content and method, spirit and technique, principles and conclusions, style and inspiration—all the elements of this elevated science about God came together to manifest the character of a new type of theology.

At the beginning of theological reasoning stands the "why," which both expresses natural curiosity and enlists the critical questioning of an adult mind. This is why the *quaestio* is the key method of scholasticism. The very word, in its most technical meaning, defines the literary form of the principal works of St. Thomas and explains their structure. The articles of the *Summa Theologiae*, with their continual *utrum* (whether) at the beginning of each, are merely a summary within a compendium of Thomas's work. The *quaestio disputata* (disputed question) is the model of his normal way of arguing and teaching. The masterpiece of Thomas's time as Master in Paris is composed of disputed questions which were much discussed in the charged atmosphere of the university in the 1250s. These were solemn assemblies in which the Master, after having announced the theme of the discussion and its major points, submitted them for hours at a time to debate with his peers. In particular, during the first three years of Thomas's time as Master in Paris, the twenty-nine questions of the *De veritate* "About Truth" (entitled from the topic of the first question) were produced in this very fashion.

Here we see how the theologian clearly reaches beyond the private articulation of his personal curiosity about the faith. As those officially qualified and mandated, theologians fulfill an ecclesial function that is of course not at the level of magisterial teaching founded on apostolic succession in the episcopate or the papacy. However, under the jurisdiction of the Church, theologians undertake research that is necessary for the spiritual refreshment of believers living in the world. There have always been masters—both in theology and in catechetics—assisting the order of bishops. They are professionals whose juridical title rightly comes from the university and not from the hierarchy. *Magistri*, the Masters in Theology, under these conditions, possess an official title to speak about faith and doctrine. They not only explain and interpret—activities that already pose some possibility of disagreement. While maintaining an orthodox fidelity to the gospel, they also construct the content of the faith in strikingly different expressions in order to articulate the implications of the relation of human beings and their world to the divine, to underline some particular aspect of divine mystery, and to balance in different ways all these factors.

This is a freedom which is very delicate and which the Church always oversees from its own perspectives of the moment. This is a sign of reason's mastery of human intelligence, even as it is expressed in religious docility. Thomas Aquinas criticized Anselm and distanced himself at times from Augustine; Thomas was going to be frequently contradicted by Bonaventure. The Master "made a determination" (as they said in that time) after listening to the various positions and discussion of the problems. The Masters were not "authorities" in the technical sense of this term: neither their situation nor their role warranted that distinction. But their work became a theological *locus*—a place where theology can be discovered—one step beneath the Fathers of the Church. Thomas Aquinas will become the Doctor of the Church *par excellence* for the Western world.

We need to add that this fearless rationality has a weakness that attaches to the nature of faith. Following its authentic role in theology, reason must keep itself within the ambiance of mystery, thus within the obscurity of this kind of knowledge, and in docility to listening to the Word of God. Theological science is marked by both this defect and by this parallel grandeur. It is a dialectic of faith wherein its strength conquers its weakness.

After all, due proportion considered, reason works as follows in the life of the spirit: it does not become complacent with its questions and its formulations, but rather develops in a normal and healthy fashion between two kinds of "knowledge"—a vital perception of an object at the outset and a delight in the object finally possessed at the end. If that is the shape of earthly understanding, how much more so must faith—in virtue of its divine object and its inner hunger—resolve all its questions and all its explorations into a simple gaze of supreme delight and ineffable communion with the divine mystery.

Theologians, having reached this goal, experience even in the rational texture of their work, the absolute transcendence of the faith. They understand that this work is constituted by truth, not by opinions addressed to no one in particular. But theological truths do not shadow the purity of God's word with human weakness. The word remains free of encumbrance in the gratuity and graciousness of revelation. Faith plays its role freely and with mastery within the concepts, the inferences, and the deductions of scholarship. Reason and its philosophy are here servants of divine teaching. The triumph of the faith lies precisely in its capacity to maintain the efficacy of reason's powers, without cheating human intelligence and without adding anything to the divine illumination.

Here is the theandric mystery of the Word of God—Word made flesh. Sanctity is required to achieve this mystery in theology. In the person of Thomas, the doctor is a saint. Understand, however, that in this case he is a saint because he is a doctor—and this doctor of the church is a doctor because he is a saint. This is the sanctity of intelligence. At the very heart of the spirituality of Thomas Aquinas rests this conviction: human understanding is a place for holiness, because the Truth is holy.

TEXTS

A Eulogy of Theology

One day Simonides wanted to persuade one of his friends to abandon his search for God and to concentrate on human concerns, saying that humans ought to concern themselves with things at their own level. Let human beings find delight in humans; let mortals be preoccupied with mortal realities. To this Aristotle retorted: on the contrary, human beings ought to lift themselves up as far as they can to immortal and divine realities. Of course they can perceive but little, but this little is more worthy of love and desire than the knowledge of lower things. In fact, in addressing the problems of the universe, if only by provisional hypotheses, our intellectual powers are quite significant.

From these observations of Aristotle it appears that an imperfect knowledge of superior realities confers on the soul a supreme perfection. Confronted with what transcends its reason, the human spirit cannot be at that same level; but when we are dealing with even a poor grasp of the faith, this holds open to us already a high perfection.

. . . Human reason finds access to these truths of faith by way of analogies, truths which will become perceptible only in the vision of God. There is nothing here that will allow for demonstrations or for proofs. But, setting aside presumption, the human mind still takes extreme delight in these weak reasonings and these limited reflections.

. . . You might say that we are cutting the strong wine of wisdom with water—cutting the wine of the Word of God with the water of human reason, and that this mixture spoils the wine. But no, not if you are a good theologian; for then, it is not the wine which is cut with water, but the water which is changed into wine, as at the wedding feast of Cana.

. . . In his book on the Trinity, Hilary praises this questing: "In your faith, strive, make progress, plod on! You will not arrive at your goal, I know, but the least progress toward it is already full of grace. Anyone who pursues the infinite with zeal makes progress, even if they do not arrive all the way to the end. All the same, refrain from claiming to penetrate the mystery through this immersion in a truth that is without boundary; the primary condition for progress is to understand that truth surpasses all comprehension."

Summa contra Gentiles, Book I, ch. 5 and 8;
Commentary on Boethius de Trinitate, q. 2, art. 3, resp. 5.

On Wisdom and Science

Theology is the supreme act of human intelligence: it is the wisdom among the sciences. St. Thomas has recourse here to categories borrowed from Greek philosophy (already used by St. Augustine in a very different way) in order to articulate the dignity of theology. For Augustine, wisdom (with its supreme divine object and its unique method) diminished the human sciences, which he saw as condemned to fragile and passing interests. Yet St. Thomas allots to these sciences their full dignity and their autonomous methodology. Within his system, they promise rational certitude according to the pursuit of the proper formal object of each science. The human sciences have wisdom figures at their own level of endeavor (see ch. 5, below).

The science of theology is not diminished by this autonomy of the human sciences. Theology's eminence derives from the fact that, in the great order of knowledge and of causes, theology treats of God as its object, i.e., treats of the supreme Cause of both the beginning and the end of all things. It is exactly the transcendent nature of its object that accounts for its weak epistemological condition—as the following text suggests: in the face of the unattainable mystery of the divine, theology hangs on to the assent of faith given on the authority of the Word of God.

Popular use, which is the norm for the meaning of words, calls *sages* those who are charged to put order into things and to govern them well. So among the attributes that people confer on the truly wise, Aristotle declares that it pertains to them to be the agents of order.

Since our interest here is to guide and order all things to their final end, it is clear that we will need to draw the rule for their guidance and their ordering from the end itself. Each thing is perfectly constructed when it is appropriately ordered toward its correct end—for the end (or goal) of each thing is its good. In this way, within the disciplines of thought and action, we consider that a discipline is directive and functions as a principle for another when it is able to assign its proper end to that other. In this way the art of medicine guides pharmacy and directs it so that health (which is the object of medicine) becomes the end of the pharmaceutical arts. Likewise, in the building of ships, the art of piloting is directive; or in chivalry and its apparatus for combat, the military art takes the directive role.

Similarly in the sciences, some are directive and are called architectonic (or architectural) because of their function of serving as a principle. For this reason, their theorists, whom we can call architects, are justly called truly wise. But because in each branch these architects set the ends (or goals) of each of the disciplines without however directing them to the supreme goal of all knowing, they are wise relative to a particular area only. The title "wise" *par excellence* is reserved for those who consider the final end of the whole universe, which is at the same time its principle (or source). So Aristotle says that it belongs to the wise to consider the supreme causes of beings.

Summa contra Gentiles, Book I, ch. 1

3: The Contemplative

At the time when he was composing his commentary on the book of Isaiah, Brother Thomas was blocked for a long time in his efforts to interpret a difficult passage. He started praying to understand the meaning of the text. And one night Reginald, Thomas's secretary who was resting in the cell next to his Master's, heard what sounded like a conversation. At the end of it, Thomas called Reginald: "Get up. Bring some light. Get the notebook for today and get ready to write." Then, for an hour, as if reading from an open book, Thomas dictated to his secretary his commentary on the passage from Isaiah whose interpretation had previously been hidden to him. When he had finished, Thomas sent his faithful companion back to bed."[1]

This scene as described by his biographer is wonderfully suggestive—all the more so because we still possess the handwritten manuscript (Vatican, ms. lat. 9850) in which his secretary's handwriting transcribes the words of his Master. Here we can see how St. Thomas's technical work developed coherently from religious and contemplative inspiration as well as from his careful technical treatment of the sacred text (the font of his theological work). Following what we have just said, it is clear that for Thomas Aquinas contemplation is the beginning and the end of his life—of his "state of life" as he would have put it—as well as of his theology. In defining the structure and the rules of contemplative life, St. Thomas has revealed to us, despite the impersonal objectivity of his teaching, the secret of his own personality as much as if he had written "confessions" for us in the manner of Augustine.

[1] William of Tocco, *Vita Sancti Thomae Aquinatis*, ch. 31 in Prümmer, ed., *Fontes vitae S. Thomae Aquinatis* (St. Maximin, 1924) 105.

Thomas Aquinas by Fra Angelico.

THE THEOLOGICAL AND EVANGELICAL ASPECTS
OF CONTEMPLATION

First we need to retrieve the word contemplation from too facile a usage and identify its root meaning as St. Thomas sees it. Contemplation is an act of a life lived with God in faith, that is, of divine life as we participate in it through the theological virtues of faith, hope, and charity. Contemplative life is nothing other than the combined exercise of these three divine energies. This understanding allows us to situate it both psychologically and doctrinally beyond the rites and acts of "religion," whether individual or communal. The nature and structure of contemplation will make this clear.

By defining religion as a virtue which renders the worship due to God, St. Thomas points out with balanced clarity both the scope and the limits of the kind of relationships that religion establishes between us and God. Divine worship expresses our awareness of our condition as creatures. Our religious acts take on a sort of cosmic amplitude through their submission to divine sovereignty. Religious supplicants place themselves before the Creator at the heart of the universe, of which they acknowledge God to be the source. In religious acts, these vast feelings are expressed in rituals that engage our senses; cosmic and human realities, body and soul, are here brought together. This kind of relationship to our divine destiny expresses one of the greatest capacities of our human spirit. Religious submission is fundamentally an expression of the greatness of the human spirit.

However vacillating our consciousness of our radical dependency on the divine might be in certain cases—clouded by myths, encumbered by superstitions, or perverted by alienation—even when religion grasps divine reality only superficially through a completely sense-bound emotionality, it still reaches by its nature beyond human interests and beyond the world. Religious expression discovers in the secret depths of being and of life a dimension where the sense of what we call the *sacred* can be recognized.

Christian contemplation, on the other hand, is rooted in divine faith and is of a very different caliber. Even where contemplation must take responsibility for the actions and environment of worship, it operates in another frame of reference than that of religion. St. Thomas without hesitation makes religion—the virtue dealing with worship—a moral virtue. As a moral virtue, religion's object is to relate the meaning of our life to the divine, whereas it belongs to contemplation to perform acts that participate in divine life itself and lead us to a connatural experience of God. Thomas Aquinas astonished some of his hearers when he took his cue from Cicero in locating religion and its whole expression of cult under the category of justice.

Justice is the virtue governing appropriate exchange. Not that God owes anything at all to creatures, nor even that creatures could ever repay adequately their debt to God, since they have received the entirety of their being gratuitously! But creatures are obliged to fit themselves into a relationship with God, and their awareness of their incapacity to do this becomes itself the homage and service that they offer to their Lord. This is a fundamental need of an intelligent creature. It is expressed in religiously sensitive societies through the duty to fulfill laws governing worship. It is expressed as well by the awareness of individuals who become conscious that they owe everything to God.

In light of this, it is evident that the contemplative instinct generated by a living faith belongs to a different order of reality than religion. Of course, for believing Christians, it can be difficult to distinguish between the worship that they offer to God (acts of the virtue of religion), and those which arise from the theological virtues

Autograph handwriting of Thomas Aquinas from his Commentary on Isaiah.

of faith, hope, and charity. The same God to whom we offer homage in ritual and to whom we speak in prayer is the God of our faith and our love. The God of religion is the same personal God who reveals himself and who speaks to the heart of those who humbly listen to him. This is not just the God who is the Author of nature, but the God of Abraham, Isaac, and Jacob, the God of history who, in Jesus Christ, reveals himself as Father.

When God's mercy and friendship are revealed to us as the real abundance of sheer generosity that they are, we are overwhelmed: our religious feeling reaches a high point, and we can only respond with the gift of our heart. The more God is revealed to us in a communion of life, the more this feeling of God's being "totally other" grows. We become vividly conscious of the disproportion between Creator and creature in the very midst of an experience of unity. Even the most childlike trust carries with it a rush of emotion at being so greatly loved. But the point is this, that religion in its exterior worship and its interior oblation is dilated and as it were straightaway transported onto another plane (without putting our indebtedness to God out of the picture). It becomes no longer a question of living *for* God, but of living *in* God—or better, living a divine life. No more is the issue how properly to relate to God (which always remains a fact of life, of course), but how to commune with God.

Will the contemplative then discount ritual experiences and the observances of worship to which religion invites us? Of course not. Thomas Aquinas could not forget his adolescence at Monte Cassino. But the experience of contemplative life will caution Christians against a certain unnatural exaggeration of the virtue of religion (especially organized as highly structured social expectations) to which monasticism gave in at times.

A contemplative attitude will guard against a complacency that could allow a monk, caught up in his rites of adoration, to ignore the social distress of human groups (in a prematurely imagined Heavenly City). Monasteries would still teach the poor folk, give them the sacraments, provide them a sacred world to live in. But in such a version of Christianity, there is not the same passion to evangelize, to proclaim the Good News out of Christian fraternal love.

Yet charity is the inspiration and the rule of everything in the Christian life. No one better than the one whose life is the contemplation of God knows how charity is expressed in all its forms. Out of the heart of contemplative love, all the high sentiments that characterize the "religious" soul are secretly expressed. There is a keen experience of the transcendence of the Father in the deep experience of his mercy. At the same time, great apostolic vocations arise out of this contemplative experience, awakening sensitivity to human misery and hope for its relief as an expression of the gospel's power.

Observe how far we are from the religion of fear, from its social conformity, from its separation from ordinary life, from its ritual legalism, and from any kind of moralism. Here we are describing "religion in spirit and in truth" where the freedom of the children of God overcomes the enslavement of the Law. This freedom, moved by love, consents to the total gift of self in a moral responsiveness greater than ever. In no way are we talking about setting aside divine and human laws; but we can observe a break with a certain way of understanding them. "Worship in spirit and in truth": this gospel reference (John 4:23-24, at the end of Christ's conversation with the Samaritan woman) in fact represents a turning away from the ritual apparatus of the Old Covenant—away from the absolutism of the Law which would have rejected any dialogue with that ungodly Samaritan woman. The faithful one of the New Covenant "fulfills" the Old, and his faith is still the faith of Abraham. But this fulfillment of God's promises in Christ (in this joining of the human and the divine) doesn't come about without a break from the past.

From now on, in the Son of God made man (after our human likeness), we are adopted children; and the God of Sinai is truly called Father. From now on, we have left behind the culture of submission under the yoke of the Law with its external demands written on stone tablets and its defensive prohibitions against the "Gentiles." From now on, if there is law, it is the law of faith given by the inner testimony of the Spirit. Precepts do no more than prepare the heart, and their written formulation is of secondary importance. Formulations and precepts would even be deadly, if they were to predominate in the style of directives given by teachers to children. We are now adults at an age to love—the age of perfection, the age of freedom; we have moved beyond the apparatus of observances. This "new" law, of course, is the law of the gospel.

Nowhere in the texts of Thomas are the words of the gospel—the gospel of Christ and the evangelizing of Paul—as adequately expressed as in this teaching about the "new law." Here we recover explicitly and with theological insight the revolutionary inspiration that defined the apostolic and spiritual initiative of the Friars Preachers and the Friars Minor. The impact of this gospel inspiration caused a change of direction in the observance of religious practices, breaking away from the established order of monasticism at the very time when the splendor of Cluny had exploded into magnificent ritual expression and into its theocratic political influence. Francis of Assisi had consciously set aside the Rule of St. Benedict and, as one poor for the sake of Christ, had renounced the political and religious influence that monasticism had engendered. St. Dominic had resituated the choral office to become a "means" in the service of the apostolic end.

Both of these decisions will have their effect on the relativizing of solemn liturgy (the *opus Dei* that was supreme in the life of the monk) and on the de-absolutizing of the Rule by the principle of dispensation. For the friars, the supreme works of their life are fraternal love and contemplative faith, both as experienced and as communicated; nothing else bears the same weight of importance. Love and contemplative faith are the unique divine exercises that lead to evangelical perfection, sketching here on earth a glimpse of the beatific vision and of the universal fraternity of heaven. By contrast, religion expresses our debt as creatures, whether through personal devotion or public rites. So religion is only the material locus of our acts of faith and of love. Thomas Aquinas pronounced the principle that he carried out in his own life as the realization of the primitive gospel: *There is no greater sign of love than to enter into contemplation.*

CONTEMPLATION AND ACTION

The word *contemplation* is not in the Gospels, and the "knowledge" of John's Gospel (cf. John 10:14f.) is something entirely different from the *theoria* of the philosophers. To the surprise of many, St. Thomas used a vocabulary, a method, and an interpretation in his analysis of the primitive spirit of the Friars Preachers that remind us immediately of the Greek origin of his terminology. The Greek philosophers were the geniuses who, working from reason, defined contemplation as the supreme activity of human beings. But their ancient Greek context was vastly different from that of the gospel reality and its *vita apostolica*. In the mendicant revolution of the twelfth and thirteenth centuries, the distinction between action and contemplation in human acts and in the states of life became very important.

We should understand that when St. Thomas defines Dominican life as "mixed"—a life where contemplation and action belong together, united despite the distinction of their specific acts—he introduces doctrinal categories that are the product of human reasoning. Here in his articulation of his spiritual ideal, we find him doing what he does throughout his theological work. The distinction between nature and grace comes into play within (and for the benefit of) an integration of faith and reason. Gospel faith brings rational analysis into play in order to clearly explain itself and to take full account of its human significance.

Thomas Aquinas the preacher is faithful to Dominic's gospel inspiration in defining himself as a contemplative. Furthermore, the Christian spiritual tradition that distinguishes between the contemplative life and the active life as two distinct types arose from the influence of Gregory the Great, the spiritual master of the Western Fathers second in rank only to Augustine, who introduced these categories from Greek humanism and expressly applied them to Christian spirituality.

Out of this came a copious tradition about contemplation, supple in its variant expressions coming from monastic as well as other sources. St. Thomas brought all these contributions to bear in support of his teaching, after having first applied them to his own religious experience.

"Pride goes before a fall." [left] "Humility." [right] From the Sketchbooks of Villard de Honnecourt, *a contemporary of Aquinas.*

His brilliant analysis will assure for this teaching its stature as a classic. However, the success of these ideas will pay the price of attracting uninspired imitators once this great insight became widely known. Yet revivals of gospel spirit in the Church throughout the centuries repeatedly restored the theme to its primitive purity of expression.

We should carefully observe the context for the change that the idea of contemplation undergoes. Because contemplation is lifted up into the mystery of divine communion in the gospel, the contemplative becomes substantially transformed in ways that St. Thomas attentively describes. In doing so, he draws upon both the general experience of Christians and (doubtless) his own experience. We would be making a great mistake if we were to detect only scholastic subtlety in these texts where he makes a radical distinction between the contemplation of the philosopher and the contemplation of the believer. The elevation of the soul and the intelligence into a new sphere of faith experience is not a matter of only minor significance. Within the context of faith, the object of contemplation is no longer just the divinity as the cradle of ideas and the first cause of beings, but my Father who is God and whose loving initiative has introduced me into his living mystery.

The contemplative gaze, without losing the intellectual character which the Greek philosophers described for it, is nonetheless the effect of a vital communion within which the principle of knowing has become the gift of love. The delight that we experience here comes not only from the discovery of the truth, but from the joy of experiencing the goodness of God. It is love for the divine Object that absorbs our attention, rather than our hunger for knowledge about God. "Although it is a delightful thing to be able to see; it is even more delightful—another thing altogether—to see one whom we love," as Aquinas says.

The Latin and French languages have only the one word *veritas/vérité* to name the object of two kinds of knowledge that are very different. Some other languages (Slavic, for example, as well as biblical Hebrew and Greek) profit from more supple vocabulary. Especially in his biblical commentaries, St. Thomas had to create a repertory of complementary expressions to do justice to the meaning of the Scriptures in his description of contemplation, without succumbing to pious rhetoric in the process.

In this context of biblical sources, Thomas inaugurates a critique of moralism (the attitude that human perfection consists in good behavior), based on his correct understanding of the tight coherence between action and contemplation. Just as the gospel is not proclaimed first of all to put either individual or public morality in good order, but rather to reveal God's love for sinners; in similar fashion, divine contemplation does not have as its purpose to lead individuals to make good resolutions or to live up to the duties of their state in life. Contemplation has an absolute value as the object of full human delight, beyond questions of morality and even in the midst of the sordid reality of sin. Remember to whom Christ announces the need for "worship in spirit and in truth"—he speaks to the much-married Samaritan woman. St. Thomas's commentary on that text is perhaps the most splendid exposé that he ever gave about the transcendence of faith.

But, we might ask, by so exalting contemplation, does he give in to the intellectualism of the Greeks? Does Thomas's attitude support the idea (unacceptable for a Christian) that the sage is an aristocrat of the spirit whose social privileges are paid for by the servitude of "mechanical arts" (as they were called in the middle ages and even down to the seventeenth century), that is, by the unfortunate labor of those condemned to work with material objects as contrasted with the "liberal" arts? Not the case: we are cornered into the gospel-inspired reversal of values just defined by St. Thomas. Contemplation is from this point on the privilege of the humble who in the purity of their faith are rendered interiorly apt to penetrate the mystery of God. "Happy the pure of heart, for they shall see God."

So paradoxically in Thomas's writings, the Greek spirit is used to defend the claims of the gospel, in contrast to the pastoral pietism and the moralizing upon the beatitudes of his predecessors. As Aristotle said, the moral virtues are no more than the predisposition for human perfection that comes through contemplation. The virtues can even be an earth-bound obstacle to happiness by reason of their ascetical struggle. Their equilibrium, even when achieved, never reaches to the *kalos kagathos* (the perfect moral character of Aristotle's ethics), since the beauty of the virtues is only "borrowed":

"Beauty is discovered principally and essentially in the contemplative life and in contemplative understanding, whose prerogative it is to provide illumination for the rest of life and to develop our being according to its proper proportions. So *Wisdom* says of the contemplation of wisdom: 'I have fallen in love with beauty' (*ST,* II–II, q. 180, art. 2, resp. 3)."

The beatitudes of the gospel reach beyond the scope of virtue; they are not the subject matter for commandments. They flow from a new life. Isn't the beatitude of the pure of heart something entirely different from the reasonable healthfulness of those who are temperate? And isn't the beatitude of the poor more than careful use of earthly goods? Poverty is the beloved fiancée of Francis of Assisi. And in the structure which Thomas creates for the *Summa Theologiae,* he places the beatitudes after his treatment of the virtues—beyond matters of precept— as the first taste of the beatific vision and of the fulfillment of love.

Thomas is unique in doing this. His choice was abandoned by others, who relegated the Beatitudes of the Sermon on the Mount to considerations outside of their systematic theological concerns. Such authors failed to claim the Beatitudes as the supreme expression of the contemplative and evangelical nature of theology. Their theology was reserved for the pragmatic moralism of a de-intellectualized spirituality.

With Aquinas, Greek intellect becomes uncoupled from its aristocratic associations. As a preacher, Thomas re-imagines the Greek dualism action/contemplation. He surmounts this division that is constitutive of the human condition and its woes. He describes the structure of a unified life which he calls "mixed": here action flows out of the abundance of contemplative experience in such a way that, under the structuring guidance of contemplation and by force of its unifying power, this "mixed" life is understood to be superior to pure contemplation.

A spiritual dialectic stretches the soul of the Preachers: pulled one way by contemplation, another by apostolic passion, their interior life, even their freedom, is at issue. Saint Thomas allows us to understand that he is speaking about his own experience when he says:

"There are some who experience in the contemplation of God such delight that they are unwilling to let go of it, even for the service of God in the salvation of their brothers and sisters. There are others, however, who arrive at such a summit of love where even this divine contemplation, in which they experience the greatest delight, is re-expressed in serving God in their brothers and sisters. That was the perfection of the Apostle Paul. That is the perfection that belongs to the preachers."[2]

In reading this text, we can't resist seeing the personal experience of Thomas Aquinas as he puts the attraction to pure contemplation in

[2] *Quaestio disputata de caritate,* art. 11, resp. 6.

its proper place next to the more eminent evangelizing act of the Friar Preacher. Wasn't this, after all, the initial intuition of his vocation? This disciple of Aristotle is first of all a son of Saint Dominic.

This transformation of the Greek dualism between *theoria* and *praxis* can only be fully achieved through the preacher's passion for the gospel. There our human love for others is the same thing as Christ's love for our brothers and sisters. No humanism achieves this unity in which a passionate desire for the salvation of the world flows out of a living experience of God incarnate. We see here two sides of the same mystery of the humanity of God.

Within this mysticism, as in all true mysticism, *praxis* is no longer external to *theoria,* nor *theoria* valid without *praxis.* The Christian—a *vir evangelicus,* as St. Dominic was called—finds completeness in the *vita apostolica,* which is not just the juxtaposition of action and contemplation, but rather "the truth and the life" of St. John (cf. John 14:6). Faith's purpose is not to satisfy spiritual curiosity (even a curiosity famished for the experience of God), but rather to direct us toward our ultimate goal in and through Christ. This realistic reading of the gospel keeps us firmly within the concrete economy of salvation and protects us from adopting nonhistorical ideas of salvation. Human philosophies cannot bring about this unity of contemplation and action.

Theology in St. Thomas's hands creates an organic structure for the content of this truth: it is a wisdom that is at once both contemplative and active. Of course, contemplation and action emerge from different "disciplines"; but the modern distinction between dogma and morality finds no support within the spirituality and methodology of the *Summa.* Likewise, the distinction between the ascetical (action) and the mystical (contemplation) breaks down before the unity of the grace of Christ.

The chronicler has related for us an incident about the prayer of Brother Thomas the contemplative who, the night before his inaugural lecture as a young Master in Paris (March 1256), experienced a kind of anguish while preparing his first course. He prayed: "Save me, Lord; I am going down among the children of men where your truths have been smashed to bits." *Salva me, Domine, quoniam diminutae sunt veritates inter filios hominum*" (Psalm 11/12).[3] Here we can see

---

[3] William of Tocco, op. cit., ch. 16, 85. The text of the inaugural lecture is presented among the texts at the end of this chapter. See pp. 59–60.

the wrenching of his spirit away from contemplation and back toward the work to which he vowed his life.

The handing on of the truth calls for the involvement of the whole person. Teaching is a work of the active life.[4] Contemplation dominates the equation, of course. But the contemplative life remains united with the apostolic because of the very character of the action: communicating divine truth means, in a sense, not abandoning it, but rather remaining lovingly attached to this truth that is intimately assimilated and possessed. The image of Jacob's Ladder on which the angels ascend and descend suggests this ideal.[5] It is likewise expressed in the famous formula, *contemplata aliis tradere* (to give to others the fruits of contemplation).[6]

This has to be properly understood, however. This profound unity of contemplation and action in the exercise of apostolic life presupposes an orientation for contemplation different from that of a purely speculative thinker. At the heart of Christian contemplation we find not a love of pure ideas, but rather a love of God and of our brothers and sisters. The apostolic vocation arises directly out of a love troubled by others' needs. Likewise, the idea of the "mixed" life is not that of a detached philosopher who leaves his leisurely speculation to offer a new theory to his contemporaries, nor that of a poet who sings about sublime insights, as if to say: *Let those fathom this who wish to; let those understand who can.* This would be a gross misunderstanding of *contemplata aliis tradere* ("handing on what is contemplated to others"). The contemplation of the apostle, arising from a love for others that desires to help them, understands itself as completely oriented toward the spiritual destitution to which it feels that it must respond. The apostle simply has to enter profoundly into the experience of God. Ascending and descending Jacob's Ladder without ceasing, the apostle mediates contemplative experience to communicate it effectively—a loving labor of adapting divine mystery to human situations.[7]

[4] "Docere est opus activae vitae": *Summa Theologiae*, II–II, q. 181, art. 3.

[5] This is a traditional allegorical theme borrowed from St. Gregory and used by writers, teachers, and artists in the Middle Ages. The angels, coming and going from God to creatures and from creatures back to God are nonetheless not deprived of their enjoyment of the contemplation of God through their ministry on earth. Cf. *Summa Theologiae*, II–II, q. 181, art. 4, resp. 2.

[6] *Summa Theologiae*, II–II, q. 188, art. 6.

[7] Jean Mennessier, "Vie contemplative et vie active," in *Initiation Théologique*, vol. III (Paris: Cerf, 1952), ch. 18, 1125.

THE STRUCTURE OF THE SOUL AND MYSTICAL EXPERIENCE

In this same context, St. Thomas offers us his decisive understanding of the structure and dynamics of theological contemplation, a topic for which his Dominican life furnished him the actual experience. Here again, the impersonal objectivity of his doctrine should not hide the implications for how he experienced this in his own life.

Should St. Thomas be considered a mystic? Because of various problems with unfortunate theological expressions, the history of the use of the word *mystic* hides ambiguities that are hard to cut through. The categories ascetical/mystical as also the dichotomy scholastic/mystical have been among the most destructive. Such dichotomies are foreign to the language and the thought of St. Thomas. Even clever wordplay fails to make them fit within the historical heritage of Thomism.

Such words certainly convey valid ideas at an empirical level, where their pedagogical usage can be understood. However, they are unable to describe adequately contemplation and its impact on graced humanity. The analysis that Thomas provides is evidently not what the "schools of spirituality" describe in their dogmatic explanations. Thomas's analysis arises out of a theological wisdom whose criteria for truth, even when related to mystical experiences authenticated by the Church, are linked to the dynamics of faith.

According to St. Thomas, divine life is not laid over the surface of our understanding like an external additive; rather it is infused at the root of our being. Divine life is built up in us according to the framework of our nature, even as it surpasses our nature ontologically. We can say that grace is within us after the fashion of a *(super)*nature; that is to say, after the fashion of a principle most interior to ourselves, most our own, at the same time that it is divine. It is the dynamic force of grace that makes us capable of living communion with God. From grace arise the virtues, whose role is to enable us organically—in all our activities—to conduct ourselves as children of God. Faith, hope, and charity are called "theological" virtues, precisely because they, first of all, give us the capacity to live this divine life.

Faith, as we said, is the apt organism for contemplation, moved as it is by the urging of love and existing in the tension of hope. Contemplation, either as an act or as a way of life, can be understood as gathering into unity all the ways of participating in divine life. It is completely different from a metaphysical search for God or from an exploration for the first cause of and ultimate reason for the world. It is a person-to-person relation based on the realism of the gospel's witness to God-made-man; contemplation is the continuation in human history of this mystery realized in the life of the Church. The contemplative realizes and feels the claim of St. John: "Those who abide in love, abide in God and God in them" (1 John 4:16).

These are the elements and values involved in this mutual indwelling whose portrait St. Thomas constructs not only from a psychological, but from a theological perspective as well. In this taking possession of one by the other, the engagement of the affections envelops the intellect's act (distinct from the act of loving) with fervor and delight. In a parallel way, affectivity itself becomes transformed into a kind of intelligibility by the mediation of the object that is loved. Love, of course, does not grasp its object without the mediation of knowledge. Love is not itself knowledge, nor does love become knowledge. But the loved object reflects, so to speak, the impulse of love that moves to embrace it. Thus love flows back upon knowledge through the characteristics that it bestows upon the object of knowing, rendering the object more conformed, more proportioned, more united to the person who contemplates. Therefore love penetrates the known object in order to enrich it intellectually and to open it to new depths under the contemplative gaze.

This is a love that gazes. In this experience the soul becomes passive at that secret point from which its highest activity springs forth. The soul experiences the attraction from the loved one (in this case the Ineffable) to which it responds in love. The soul recognizes in that Other—beyond what it can ever embrace by its intellect—the One whose vision alone can completely quiet its yearning. This is the *passio divinorum* (submission to divine actions), to use the words of the Eastern mystic Denis, an expression that St. Thomas used with satisfaction.

Faith is the organ of assent to divine truth formulated in human terms. Yet in this kind of experience, the normal rhythm of the virtue of faith is in a way surpassed. Love, which remains unsatisfied until it can become one with the whole reality of the beloved, flows back upon knowledge and thus elevates the light of faith lifting it toward an apprehension of the Ineffable. This intimate penetration of knowledge by love is incapable of being adequately conceptualized, even in the language of faith. Here is an apprehension that will form inside us an operation of the Holy Spirit (God's own personal Love). This experience is not an activity added on top of the life of grace, but rather the achievement and completion of the vital movement that love arouses in our human spirit.

In order to locate this unique activity within the structures of our supernatural life, St. Thomas has recourse to a term that is traditional in Christian language and experience and that is also rooted in biblical categories. He calls it a "gift" of the Holy Spirit. Theologians before him had treated these gifts as spiritual categories, naming them in a variety of ways that were more or less satisfactory. St. Thomas gave them both their proper role and their full significance at the apex of the divine organism of grace. The gifts are powers that arise from the Holy Spirit. They are called "gift" precisely because they result from the gratuitous grace that follows upon the free attraction of two loves spontaneously united. This gift is however a power organically seated in the agent, not an exceptional moment like a passing tornado before which I lose composure and self-control.

These gifts—whose manifestations are psychologically described and classified under seven received categories—become a normal and integrating part of our moral life. Without diminishing the unity of the moral life, the gifts play upon two registers of operation. Faith, hope, and charity maintain their directive role, bringing about union with God, even though the Spirit's impulse relaxes the rigidity of their structure as virtues and surpasses their rational characteristics. Love cannot be satisfied with structure; the Holy Spirit cannot be made a prisoner of rationality. Here we discern the freedom of the Spirit: the theologian's eye detects here not only personal religious experience, but also texts of the Gospels and the Pauline letters that highlight a pentecostal atmosphere that transcends the realm of precepts and their virtuous constraints through the ordinary exercise of the gifts of the Holy Spirit.

It is a curious thing to note how once again St. Thomas has recourse to Aristotle to explain the infrastructure of the gifts of the Holy Spirit. The Greek philosopher had already made note of persons blessed by "fortune" who succeeded in life without the aid of reason (or even virtue) by following a happy instinct rooted in their physiology. This is a strange exception to the norm, observed the moral rationalist Aristotle, where a weakness of rationality is linked to an outburst of vitality coming from the very core of spiritual energy in the person. Aristotle, without invoking any theological principle of transcendence, nonetheless names this exception a "divine instinct." St. Thomas happily makes good use of this pagan insight in order to ground the supernatural resources of the gifts of the Holy Spirit in human nature, moving them beyond the rational conditions of our human acts.

To convey the originality of these gifts, the contrast has often been used between the sailor who tends his sail to let the gift of the wind fill it and carry it forward, on the one hand; and the virtuous rower, on the other hand, who is forced to maintain the same laborious and calculated activities. Who could miss the power of this suggestion (as well as the limits of the comparison): here St. Thomas's Aristotelian analysis informs us about the mode in which the human person is moved by grace. This is a beautiful example of theologizing which some thinkers, stuck at the level of the imagery, have condemned as naturalism.

Affected by both social and ecclesial influences, spiritualities developed over the centuries which were oblivious of the anthropological architecture which Thomas had described. They were the result of a different theology of grace, of an almost pathological fear of mystical ambiguity, and were also in reaction against the interiority of Protestant pietism. Such spiritualities accounted in completely different ways than Aquinas did for the human and divine aspects of the life of grace. Categories like ascetical and mystical, acquired and infused contemplation, ordinary and extraordinary graces—all subjects for fevered dispute—are not exactly useless (as we have said) for describing empirically the "graces of prayer." But such categories obscure the deep understanding and the evangelical temper that can be felt in the theology of St. Thomas.

AN OBJECTIVE SPIRITUALITY

We would not hesitate to describe as the "interior life" these spiritual conditions where contemplation, as the first stage of the beatifying vision of God, elicits and expresses the mystery of hidden divine communion. Certainly we couldn't explain the absolute interiority of the presence of God better than by this exalted Thomistic conception of the organism of grace. *Intimior intimo meo* (God is more intimate to me than I am to myself): this saying of St. Augustine fits perfectly the experience and the theology of St. Thomas, for whom mystical passivity is in fact the apex of the Spirit's action. From this it becomes clear that God's activity is not conceived as some sort of intervention in my personal endeavors, but rather as a creative presence introduced at the root of my existence and as an ontological spring from which my freedom flows under the power of grace.

The expression "interior life," however, carries certain equivocal connotations. The history of that expression reveals a significant shift from the original orientation of Catholic spiritual teaching; further, it is foreign to the characteristic language used by St. Thomas. If there is one decisive feature in Aquinas's spiritual teaching, it is the primacy that he gives in the analysis of psychological structures to the consideration of *objects* in order to situate the powers of the soul and define their virtues.

Neither great human effort, the renunciation of desire, strong affectivity, or interior states of the soul is the controlling value of the spiritual life. The supreme value is our positive attachment to the realities in which we find our true good, the divine realities to which virtue makes possible a right relationship for us. Psychological phenomena, marked by strong feelings and introspection, remain a secondary factor. Neither grace nor the presence of God falls within that kind of heightened psychological consciousness. The experience of the gifts is in no way essentially linked to any special psychic phenomenon.

The descriptions that the great spiritual figures of the sixteenth century have left us of their experiences are admirable theological material. However, they should not be allowed to encourage a psychological perspective that would imagine virtue to operate by effort of the will and with difficulty, or to see the goodness of an action derive from its response to a precept, or to make conscience calculate the right by way of probabilities, or to have the good order of a community rest upon authoritarian decrees, or to reduce faith to an act of obedience, or to measure the quality of love on the basis of merit. Of course, virtuous dynamics, such as temperance and courage, are brought to bear for the good of the moral agent. By cultivating these virtues in order to discipline the passions, virtuous persons make themselves the object of their acts in their concern to be good and to reach integrity. But all that is only the preparation for a higher undertaking: we can't remain complacent in attaining excellence as moral subjects. That moral strength assures us the freedom to go on to attain the objects that expand the person to divine proportions, surpassing every human measure.

Here is how we can begin to understand the theological virtues. God becomes the object of our acts—to the degree that we can use such a word to designate a Being who is actually unable to become an object in juxtaposition to another subject who is a creature. But we understand what is meant, for everything that we have said about life in God, theology included, would be devastated if this theologically conceived life did not possess objectivity from the outset. Whether considering our adherence to the word of God, our certitude about its saving designs, our loving delight in participating in God's beatitude, or the divine solidarity of all persons—for all of these, interior recollection is clearly the essential condition, in the long effort to achieve moral perfection of the soul. But perfection and recollection are imperated (called forth) by the same divine objects with whom the soul has entered into communion.

This objectivity becomes clear if we observe the equilibrium of contemplatives. If they become centered on their "interior life," they are then tempted to underestimate the virtues that focus on external acts out of their desire to maintain a state of silence and peace. But they would then lose touch in their solitude not only with their passionate impatience for the salvation of the world, but with the human condition itself. Human solidarity can only be conceived and realized in the midst of society, that vital environment invigorated by the whole network of the virtues organized by the virtue of justice.

According to St. Thomas, the common good is more divine than individual moral perfection. The primacy of the common good not only connects individual well-being to the community, but also makes individual behaviors objective—something which neither good intentions nor intersubjective understanding can adequately achieve. Justice, including here political justice, provides necessary parameters for fraternal love that won't be supplied by even the most fervent generosity.

Obedience is very significant as the fundamental virtue that governs all human community. Certain spiritual writers from their psychologizing tendencies treat obedience as an ascetical virtue that takes its value from and finds its norm in the very act of submission of the moral subject, assuring it perfection. For St. Thomas, obedience entails submission, of course; but for him this submission has legitimacy and value because it brings about the common good that is served by the ordered organization of human societies. This is more important than the moral perfection of the individual agent.

The underlying condition for the integrity of obedience is not a matter of acquiescence, but the service of the common good. Obedience assures the possibility of the common good—and even the will of the superior is subject to the common good. The common good, not our subjective relationship with another person who holds power, objectively grounds and illuminates our acts of virtue.

The concern to judge rightly and truly remains essential; and my superior's judgment cannot replace the judgment that I must make at the very moment that the virtue of obedience bends my will, ready and joyful, to obey the command that I receive. Neither in love, justice, or obedience does an intersubjective relationship assure either perfection or truth. The object controls my act in the freedom of the Spirit—even more so when God has become the rule of my life.

"When asked where he had learned so much, Aristotle replied: From things—which can't lie" (Aquinas, Sermon for the Second Sunday of Advent).[8]

THE CONTEMPLATIVE WITHIN THE UNIVERSE

St. Thomas's traditional source for this objective spirituality is not only the moral tradition of Aristotle, but also the Christian vision of the world that he received from the Greek Fathers of the Church. Among the latter, particularly important was Denis, that master of mysticism whose objective contemplative dialectic did not explicitly require any particular expression of an interior experience.

The human person within Denis's theology is part of nature. Within human nature, the image of God, expressed as autonomy in free will (which is the decisive element constituting the image), forms the deep core of being human. This is a source of tension as well as the foundation of our human moral structure. The norm for human spiritual growth is not first of all voluntary decision, but rather the objective expression of "a return toward the Love that is the origin of beings; itself subsisting in infinite Goodness, this Love did not want the Good to remain sterile: it moved the Good to act according to the infinite efficacy of its virtue" (Denis, *Treatise on the Divine Names,* IV, 10—a text frequently cited and commented on by St. Thomas). Union with God is not then simply the psychological effect of our efforts under grace. Rather the asceticism of our efforts is a means of realizing the depth of the ontological relationship that transforms and ennobles us. Contemplation is the motivating force for a human nature that has come forth from God and is on its way back to God.

Here we see the famous cosmic vision—the grandiose theme of all Platonic philosophies—that St. Thomas adopted even in his earliest work. While commenting on the *Sentences* of Peter Lombard, the Augustinian theology concerning psychological and historical "states"

[8] Cf. *The Homilies of St. Thomas Aquinas,* trans. John M. Ashley (Ft. Collins, Colo.: Roman Catholic Books, 1996 [orig. 1873]) 7.

was imposed upon his thought. In his *Summa Theologiae*, however, his point of departure and the plan for his synthesis of theology are expressly taken from Dionysian theology. He adopts this vision to such a point that the historic fact of the incarnation seems to some to appear only incidental to the systematic enterprise—a misunderstanding to which the gospel-inspired preacher theologian would never agree. In addition, Thomas's theology is here in accord with St. Bonaventure in using this Platonic theme. Bonaventure, his Franciscan partner in the evangelical renewal of theology, wrote his *Itinerarium mentis* ("Journey of the Soul") within the framework of the theology of Denis, even as he focused upon an analysis of texts of Augustine.

The study of morality must be placed within the context of this cosmic vision; that context justifies the demands of moral asceticism. Moral acts are in some way, through free will, facts of nature—like steps in a movement upwards. Human freedom is grounded within this sacred hierarchy of the cosmos. Love is first of all the physical reality of a virtue that seeks union with its object. Delight is the normal and life-giving ratification of any virtuous action. Ecstatic movement beyond consciousness comes not from a turning in on the self and its interiority, but rather from a surrender to the being before me. Obedience is the revelatory expression of this order within the universe. Death itself—that apparent defeat—without losing anything of its character of punishment for sin, can be explained by the physical nature of the human being that joins matter together with spirit.

We will have to describe this universe of St. Thomas more carefully. Here we are insisting, in contrast to any sort of voluntarism, upon the cosmic objectivity of the contemplative perfection of God and likewise on the freedom of the human agent in a divine (*divinissime*—says St. Thomas, following Denis) cooperation with God's rule. Observe the extraordinary liberality of a magnanimous God who achieves the omnipotence of divine "government" of the universe all the more splendidly by conferring genuine autonomous efficacy upon human creatures. *Ec-stasy:* following the etymological meaning that Denis preserves in his text, ecstasy is something quite different from the psychological marvel imagined by modern thinkers. Ecstasy is the specific act of contemplation, where *theoria* and *praxis* come together. This is totally different from either the suspension of psychic activity or from the "resolutions" coming out of a retreat. True contemplative ecstasy is human operation exactly contrary to that kind of alienation; a false spirituality is simply unable to find this true path.

TEXTS

The New Law—the Letter and the Spirit

The New Law, which is the gospel itself, is a law written in the heart. Now everything exists and is defined in terms of that in which its full power consists. So before anything else, what is most powerful in the law of the New Testament is the grace of the Holy Spirit that is given through faith in Christ. This is what the Apostle says (Rom 3:27) in calling the grace of faith the law: "So what becomes of our boasts? There is no room for them. On what principle—that only actions count? No; that the law of faith is what counts. . . ." And then he says again (Rom 8:2) "the law of the Spirit which gives life in Christ Jesus has set you free from the law of sin and death." Also Augustine says that "just as the law of works was written on tablets of stone, so the law of faith is written on the hearts of the faithful . . . and what are the laws of God written by God in our hearts other than the very presence of the Holy Spirit?" (*De Spiritu et Littera* 24, PL 44, 225).

However, the New Law also contains some secondary elements that dispose us for the grace of the Holy Spirit and some which are related to its exercise in our lives. The faithful had to be instructed about these by writing or by spoken words concerning what we must believe and what we must do.

. . . The gospel law which is given inwardly is the very grace of the Holy Spirit, and this justifies the person. . . . In its secondary elements, namely the testimony of the faith and the commandments which govern human passions and human actions, the New Law does not justify the person. "The letter kills, but the Spirit gives life," writes Paul (2 Cor 3:6). Here Augustine notes that by the *letter* is meant any written text apart from the person, even the moral precepts contained in the gospel. So even the letter of the gospel kills unless the healing grace of faith is present within the person.

ST, I–II, q. 106, a. 1 and 2

The Unifying Power of Love

The lover and the beloved may be united in two ways: there can be a real union between them when the beloved is present to the lover in actual fact. But they can also be united by affective inclination; to understand this second kind, we must look at the kind of knowledge that leads to it, since every movement of affection flows from some sort of knowledge.

There are two kinds of love—desire and friendship—that arise from two distinct ways of considering the unity between the lover and the beloved. When I have love as desire for something, I consider it as important for my betterment; but if I have love as friendship for someone, I want good things for that person as if for my own self: I then consider that person like another self. That is why a friend is said to be another self; and thus Augustine writes: "Someone did well to call his friend 'half of my soul'" (*Confessions* IV, 6; PL 32, 698).

Love is the *efficient* cause of the first kind of union because it moves us to desire and seek the presence of the beloved as someone belonging to or fitted to ourselves. Love is the *formal* cause, however, of the union of friendship, for love consists exactly in this bond. So again Augustine says that love is the unifying factor joining, or wanting to join, two beings, namely, the lover and the beloved (*De Trinitate* VIII, 10; PL 42, 960). "Joining" refers to affective union, without which there is no love; "wanting to join" refers to real union.

The feeling of mutual indwelling can be understood in terms of both cognitive and affective powers. In cognitive terms, the beloved is said to dwell in the lover insofar as the beloved is always present in the lover's thoughts, according to the phrase of Philippians, "you have a place in my heart . . . " (Phil 1:7). Reciprocally we can say that the lover is cognitionally present in the beloved in the sense that the lover is not content with a superficial knowledge, but strives to know the beloved profoundly and in every detail. Thus the lover reaches toward the interior life of the beloved. This is how it is with the Holy Spirit, who is the Love of God: 1 Corinthians 2:10 says: "the Spirit explores the depths of everything, even the depths of God."

In affective terms, the beloved is said to dwell in the lover in the sense that the beloved is constantly present in the lover's feelings. In other words, the lover delights in the beloved when present, or in good things about the beloved. When absent, the lover feels desire for the beloved in the case of love as desire; but wants good things for the beloved in the case of love as friendship. This love of friendship is not brought about by some extrinsic cause as if one wanted something in order to arrive at some other end; it is brought about rather by sheer delight in the beloved, something deeply rooted within the lover. This is why we describe love as "intimate" and speak of the "heart of love."

On the other hand, the lover also dwells in the beloved. This differs according to the type. In love as desire, the lover will not be calmed with external or superficial enjoyment of the beloved, but rather seeks to possess the beloved entirely, even what is most intimate. However, in love as friendship the lover dwells in the beloved insofar as the lover looks on the friend's fortune or misfortune—even the beloved's will—as if his or her own. It belongs to friends to will the same things and to suffer and rejoice in the same things. The lover then seems to dwell in and to identify with the beloved. On the other hand, the beloved dwells in the lover insofar as the lover wills and acts in the interests of the friend, whom the lover considers as another self.

ST I–II, q. 28, a. 1 and 2

The Gifts of the Holy Spirit

The gifts are perfections of the person superior to the virtues. The virtues ready us to respond to the moving power of reason in both interior and exterior acts. However, in order to be responsive to God's impulse in our lives, we need superior dispositions of readiness. These are called gifts, not only because they are infused (given freely) by God, but also because they render us quickly responsive to God's inspiration. In Scripture, they are spoken of as spirits rather than gifts (Isa 11:2).

. . . These are perfections of the person that render us docile before God's interior movement. Consequently, in this case, the movement of reason does not suffice and it is necessary for a movement by the Holy Spirit and also by the gifts.

Human reason receives from God two sorts of perfection: one is natural and comes from the natural light of reason; the other is supernatural and consists in the theological virtues. While this second type of perfection is greater than the first, nonetheless the first (reasonable) perfection is possessed in a more perfect way than the other. For we have full possession of the reasonable, but only an imperfect possession of the supernatural, since we love and know God imperfectly. Whoever possesses a nature, form, or power perfectly is able to act on their own according to that nature, form, or power (without however excluding God's action who acts interiorly within every nature and will). But the being who possess a nature, form, or virtue only imperfectly is not able to act on its own, but only as it is moved by another. For example, the sun gives off light by illuminating from its own power, whereas the moon, in which the principle of light is imperfectly realized, gives out light only because it is illumined. Likewise the doctor is able to practice medicine on his own from his knowledge of the art of medicine, whereas his student, not yet fully trained, cannot practice without the instructions of the doctor.

So it is with matters touching human reason, that is, things accessible to our connatural human ends. Here we can act through the judgment of reason. If God helps us with some special assistance, this comes from the superabundant goodness of God. According to the philosophers, not everyone who possessed acquired moral virtues had heroic or divine virtue. But in the order of our ultimate supernatural end, reason plays its role only as formed to some degree and imperfectly by the theological virtues; so reason's moving force is insufficient. There must further be the prompting and moving power of the Holy Spirit from on high, as Romans 8:14, 17 puts it: "All who are guided by the Spirit of God are children of God . . . and if children, then heirs."

ST I–II, q. 68, a. 1 and 2

The Freedom of the Contemplative

Do not the active life and its asceticism govern and rule the contemplative life? No! The contemplative life consists in a certain freedom of spirit. Gregory says that the contemplative life leads to a kind of liberation of the mind because it is concentrated not on temporal but on eternal realities (Homil. in Ezech. I, hom. 3, PL 76, 812). Boethius says the same: "Human souls are necessarily more free when they hold on to the contemplation of the divine Mind; but less free when they disperse themselves among corporeal matters." So it is clear that the active life does not immediately govern the contemplative life, but it does prescribe activities of the active life as dispositions for the contemplative life. So Gregory notes again: "The active life is called servitude, the contemplative life however is freedom" (Ibid., PL 76, 809).

ST II–II, q. 182, a. 1, r. 2

On the Emanation of Divine Love

Text of Denis, The Treatise on the Divine Names, ch. 4, §10

Love is itself the cause of everything. By the outpouring of its goodness, it loves all things. It makes everything. It contains everything. It achieves everything and turns everything toward its fulfillment. This Divine Eros is good, Goodness itself, pouring itself out for the sake of Goodness. Ultimately the Love that is the Giver of all being, itself subsisting in its own Good, did not choose to remain stagnant, but was moved to act according to the infinite power of its own strength.

Commentary of St. Thomas, lesson 9:

Here Denis explains how God loves. God, who is the Cause of everything, in the overabundance of divine goodness, loves everything. By way of this love, God makes every thing and bestows being upon every thing. God achieves all this, imparting to each thing the perfection that it requires as its own. God likewise has a firm hold on all reality, upholding everything in its being. God moves every thing, steering it toward God's self as its true goal. So we can say: Divine Love is good, it arises out of Goodness (which is the same thing as God-as-Loving), and it has Goodness as its object (since God loves nothing except for the motive of God's own Goodness).

To clarify further what he has said, Denis goes on to add: the Love by which God loves beings is the source of the goodness that is in them; on account of this he calls the creature's goodness the Good in expansion, because it preexists (by way of causation) in the divine Goodness. In this way every quality of perfection in creatures exists in a more excellent way in God. This is why Denis explains that Divine Love is pouring out goodness. This Divine Love has not remained contained within itself without becoming fruitful (that is, without bringing forth creatures). Rather love has moved God to create the whole panoply of being by means of the most powerful efficacy. Ultimately the very love of God's own Goodness has moved God to disseminate and communicate this Goodness to others in the ways that this is possible, that is, by way of likeness of creature to Creator. Thus God's Goodness has not remained enclosed within itself but has flowed out into others.

The Inaugural Lecture of St. Thomas (1256)

The inaugural lecture of St. Thomas at the time of his promotion to Master in the Faculty of Theology of the University of Paris in 1256 has been rediscovered and published in recent years. These are sketchy notes for a solemn and public disquisition based, in the manner of that time, upon an allegorical development of a biblical text. In this case, the text is Psalm 103/104:13—"You water the mountains, satisfying the earth with the fruit of your works." Here is an adaptation of *Thomas's Latin notes.*

The Creator and Lord established this law in his Providence, that divine gifts should reach what is lowest by way of things that are higher, according to the hierarchical order of creation.

This law applies not only to spiritual creatures, but also to bodily creatures. This is why scripture uses a metaphor taken from bodily things, namely, the image of the rain falling from the clouds and forming the rivers which in their turn give life to the earth. In the same way the divine light illuminates the minds of Masters and doctors through whose ministry this light is then passed on to the minds of students.

First, consider the profound nature of sacred teaching. This wisdom is profound because of its source, which is the word of God. . . . Next, it is profound because of the subtlety of its content. Some truths are accessible to everyone; others are understood with a great effort of reasoning. There are, however, the highest truths that transcend all human reason and can only be known through the revelation of the Scriptures. This wisdom is profound, finally, because the holy teaching addresses nothing less than the whole point of living, namely, eternal life.

Second, consider the nobility of those who teach, who are symbolized by mountains. Mountains are high, and like them the teachers of sacred doctrine are straining toward the things of heaven. . . . They are radiant: the mountains are the first to catch the sun's light, and holy teachers are the first to catch divine light in their minds. . . . They are a stronghold: like mountains which protect the surrounding countryside, holy teachers protect the faith against error. So all teachers of holy doctrine ought to be "lifted up" because of the excellent witness of their lives, incandescent in their teaching, and strong in their defense of truth. These precisely are their three functions: preaching, teaching, and disputing.

Third, the position of the hearers is symbolized in the image of the earth that is irrigated from above. These qualities are needed by the hearers: like the earth, they are solid and fruitful. Good hearers have humility or docility, a solid sense of right judgment, and fruitfulness in searching for the meaning of what they are taught and discovering how to apply it.

Fourth, there is an order in which teaching is communicated. Don't try to teach everything in one exposition, but present the teaching gradually, adapting it to the abilities of your students. Then respect the ways in which minds receive the truth. God possesses truth by nature, while the doctors merely participate in it, although abundantly. The students participate in the truth according to the limits of their hunger for it. And again: we need to respect the norms for the transmission of truth. God communicates divine truth by his own power, while the doctors are merely ministers who need to be pure of heart, intelligent, passionate, and docile. Although no one is adequate by themselves for this ministry of holy teaching, doctors can receive from God what is needed for them to be adequate.

4: The Herald of a New Christianity

Just over thirty years old, Thomas Aquinas was already fully the master of his thought and at the height of his influence. This was when Raymond of Peñafort requested that he write a work which would "bring the faith to address the errors of the infidel." Catalan by birth, Raymond of Peñafort was a great authority in the Order of Preachers and in the Church. A jurist of the highest quality and a Master in the schools of Bologna, he was already famous and middle-aged when he entered among the youngsters of the new Order of Preachers (1222) —a significant step for a man who had already devoted himself to the institutional development of the ideas of the Lateran Council (1215) that were the Church's program for renewal in the changing society. The Order of Preachers became the apt religious structure and spiritual milieu for his implementation of the Lateran Council's ideas.

Further, the fact that Raymond was haunted by the problem of the non-Christians, especially the Muslims, was not unusual for a man born in Spain, where two-thirds of the land was occupied by the Arabs. His interest in Islam sprang from both his apostolic zeal and his experience as the political counselor of princes. Besides, the Friars Preachers from the very first were anxious about the anguished situation in which Islamic expansion placed Christians with respect to both their faith and the territorial stability of Christianity.

If we accept as reliable the Chronicle of the Kings of Aragon, Thomas composed his *Summa contra Gentiles* (1258–60) in response to this intervention by Raymond, their royal counselor. However, this information is less than certain, even though it does shed light both on the origin of this masterpiece by St. Thomas as well as on the role he played in the cultural and political involvements of the Church vis-à-vis matters of both faith and culture. A Master in Theology, as we have said, was not first of all a professor in a school, even if that

St. Dominic, 1270, Florentine School.
Courtesy of Yale University Art Gallery.

school was the University of Paris, but someone who could publicly articulate gospel faith clearly for both Christian and secular contexts. In this case, we can call Thomas Aquinas a "Master in Christianity."

When in the course of 1258 this Master set up shop to begin his *Summa contra Gentiles,* Christian thinkers were already on their guard against the serious ambiguities in Aristotelian doctrines. Even Albertus Magnus, who more than fifteen years earlier had publicly declared his wish to introduce Aristotle into Christian thought, recognized the problems posed by the judicious interpretation of Aristotle's writings. This was even more important now, since the complete Aristotelian corpus was included after 1255 among the books for instruction at the university, despite earlier efforts to censor them. The many manuscripts of this corpus which we still possess bear witness, by the abundance of their interlinear and marginal glosses, to the tenacious subtlety with which rival Masters produced contrasting interpretations of the same texts.

Several interpreters, in particular the Arab philosophers, started to denounce the ambiguities in Aristotle. This was also the case with Averroes, who twenty years earlier had been called a "most noble philosopher and master of thought" by William of Auvergne, then bishop of Paris. Yet his commentaries on Aristotle became more disturbing, the more one paid attention to them. Although Averroes' interpretation of Aristotle was not yet as influential as it would be ten years later when Siger of Brabant would create the crisis of "Latin Averroism," nonetheless, the significance of this work was already evident in regard to its dangerous teachings about nature and human destiny.

This was the context for the event which would signal the start of the crisis. In 1256, Pope Alexander IV took advantage of the presence of Albertus Magnus at his papal court in Anagni to ask him to respond to Averroist doctrines about the unity of the intellect which seemed to call into question personal survival of the human individual after death. Albert, already at the height of his powers and reputation, wrote *De unitate intellectus contra Averroistas* ("On the Unity of the Intellect in Rebuttal to Those who Teach Averroes' Doctrine"). Albert was not taking on a specific teaching of Averroes here as he would have to do years later; rather he was articulating a tentative discernment about Averroism and more broadly about Arab thought out of concern about its influence following the success of Aristotle.

From here on Christianity would be forced to confront Islam on two fronts: geographical and ideological. The loosening of the Moors'

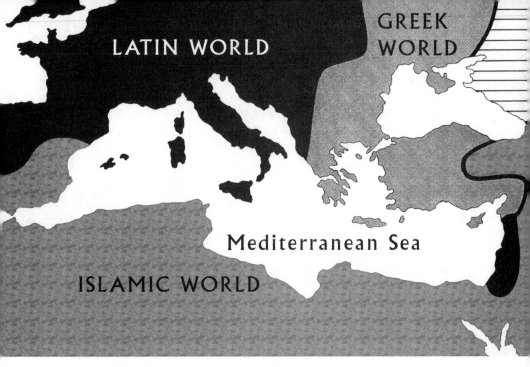

LATIN WORLD

GREEK WORLD

Mediterranean Sea

ISLAMIC WORLD

The World and Its Cultural Divisions in the 13th Century.

grip on Spain facilitated Christians' freedom of movement and made possible a missionary crusade that was not only military, but also doctrinal—a dialogue of apologetics. Arab culture was the strongest exponent of ancient Greek science and philosophy; it represented both a threat and a temptation for the Latin West. So understandably Arab writings that drew upon Greek inspiration were being discovered and translated in the Latin Christian world.

In the 1250s, a significant change of approach took place in Christianity's great strategy; its missionary efforts became linked to the crisis of high culture in a broad new approach. The *Summa contra Gentiles* has to be understood in exactly this context: the Christian missionary effort evolved into a new style because Islam showed itself to be not only a military menace, but also a culturally superior civilization. In addition, the introduction of Aristotle, thanks to Arab scholars, opened up for Christians a scientific view of the universe apart from the Bible's religious imagery. This was the singular problem that Thomas faced. How should Christians respond? He realized that it would be a mistake to separate the missionary spirit from the learning of his contemporary intellectual milieu.

Who then are these *Gentiles* (pagans)? And for whom is this *Summa* being written? Who needs to grapple with the issues of the *Gentiles?* The chronicler from Aragon suggested that the objective was to help missionaries who aimed to make headway into the Islamic world. But even from a glance, the *Summa* doesn't look much like a manual for missionaries, even a sophisticated version for encounters with Muslim elites. Both because of the wide scope of its subject matter as well as because of its method of argumentation, it evokes the ethos of a university clientele.

It might not be implausible to think, by relativizing the information given in the hagiographic account of the chronicler, that Thomas's specific intention was to address the *Summa* to the University of Paris, where the errors of the *Gentiles* (meaning the Arab philosophers) would have spread and beguiled some of the scholars. The agitation over Averroes that would lead to his condemnation in 1270 and to the long syllabus of 1277 would have already begun in the 1250s. So the *Contra Gentiles* perhaps targets and refutes the doctrines of this contemporary Averroism.

Yet it doesn't seem necessary to push the historical context back that far. In Paris in 1258 as at Rome in 1256, the objects of apologetic attention were simply some bad foreign books. The crisis over Latin Averroism was on the way, but it had not yet really begun. Furthermore, the *Summa contra Gentiles* is not specifically directed toward Averroes, but rather toward a whole company of *errantes* (mistaken authors)—including pagans, Muslims, Jews, and heretics whose works are examined and critiqued. But taking into account this nuance concerning the time needed for the influence of Averroes to grow, it should be clear that Thomas's work surpassed the character of a manual for missionaries suggested by the chronicler and saw itself rather as a defense of the whole corpus of Christian thought in the face of the Arab-Greek scientific conception of the universe that was henceforth to be a part of the Western mentality.

This brings us back once again to the importance of Paris for the world of faith. As usual, at a time of rapid change, universities are the milieu sensitive to fresh insights about urgent problems. For fifty years, teams of collaborators had been formed in the schools of Paris to deal with all kinds of issues that sometimes led to risky new frontiers. For example, John de Matha, a young Master of Paris placed in charge of the young scholars, had come up with the daring idea of founding a religious institute whose members would dedicate themselves to the liberation of captives in Muslim lands in the wake Crusades. In 1198, Pope Innocent III approved this foundatio.. new religious order (the Trinitarians), an initiative favored by the French king Philip Augustus.

This initiative was copied a bit later by a nobleman from Languedoc, Peter Nolasco, whom Raymond of Peñafort supported with both his advice and his reputation; Peter brought into existence the Mercedarians (Order of Mercy)—a company of lay knights and priests living under the Rule of St. Augustine.

Around the years 1245–50, two young Masters who were companions in scholarship, Roger Bacon and Guy Fulk, dreamed up the idea of a *respublica fidelium* (a republic of believers) drawing upon the themes of Augustine's *City of God.* Bacon, the renowned Franciscan, and Fulk who would one day be pope under the name of Clement IV, were haunted by this idea as they reflected that current ideas about Christianity were too modest for a universe that was constantly expanding. To use once again the phrase of Pope Gregory IX, Paris was certainly the oven where the whole Christian world baked its bread.

Various apostolic projects, not all of them successful, began to address these mounting problems and hopes. In 1244 there had been an expedition among the Cuman Tartars following the wave of terror caused by the Mongolian invasion of Central Europe. At that time, the Franciscans John of Plano Carpini (1246) and William of Rubruck (1254) went as far as Central Asia and dialogued with the successors of Ghengis Khan. In parallel fashion, Pope Innocent IV sent the Franciscan Lope Fernandez to be the bishop of Marrakesh and the pope's delegate to the Caliph Omar al-Murtada of the Almohad dynasty.

We will only understand St. Thomas and our reading of his work by situating him in this politically anguished yet evangelically exciting context. Thomas shaped his message based upon his motive to apply the gospel to these particular needs, without sacrificing the truth in the process. He himself did not travel to Morocco nor to Mongol lands; further, he does not even mention the Crusades. Yet he kept on his study desk the works of the great Muslim philosophers and he reckoned with new insight that Christianity, which before had been contained in the geographical and cultural forms of the Roman Empire, had really touched in fact only a part of humanity. With the help of Arab science, he began to discover the immense breadth of the universe.

The *Summa contra Gentiles* creates and applies the norms for dialogue with the "pagans," based not on tactical opportunism, but on the truth as we know it and the genuine issues of the differing perspectives. Truth itself not only takes subtle detours as we come to know it, but it also has different levels. Our assent is measured by the various methods of human thought, whose formal structures we simply must respect. As Aristotle says so well: an authentic discipline of the mind requires assent only according to the demands of the object under consideration.

Faith exercises its witness only within the confines of the mind. If the facts of nature are still largely unknown as to their exact physical properties, how much more so are the divine realities. Too easy or too pretentious an explanation would be an insult to the nonbeliever. Further, the explanations that we give need to be calculated according to appropriate norms of argumentation. With dissident believers, we can have recourse to the authority of Christ's gospel, but with Muslims and Jews we must limit ourselves to the authority of the Old Testament; while for unbelievers, reason alone—deficient though it can be in matters religious—will provide the norm and the criteria for mutual encounter.

In contrast to Muhammad, we should not put our trust in either forced assent under threat of weapons or in the seduction of earthly rewards. Rather, the decisive witness to the gospel is that, without any extraordinary signs, the world should be led to believe, by the example of ordinary and unsophisticated people, in a truth so difficult to believe, to hope for so noble a destiny, and to live a life so demanding. The example of wise figures from the past, their passion for truth and their committed quest for their true destiny, reassure us in our own quest. They are a symbol of our privilege to live with faith in the word of God.

In these polemical writings of Brother Thomas, we observe (not without a bit of self-satisfaction) his occasional impatience and the vivacity of his pen, carrying us somewhat brusquely to the center of the conflict that was then the forum for the evolution of Christian theology. Averroes should be recognized not as a commentator but a corrupter of Aristotle, protests Thomas the exegete who has attached himself to the text of the ancient Greek philosopher. But, having made note of that, Thomas then undertakes a dialogue with his adversaries that is true both to his powerful psychological insights as well as to his irenic temperament.

Thomas's method, far from excluding the thought of his opponent, examines it instead as a step in his quest for truth. His opponent can thus take his turn in the dialogue, since he stands for that part of the truth that he perceived correctly and that finds its expression integrated into a wider and more just synthesis. As his biographer described it, "Brother Thomas refutes an adversary in the same way you instruct a disciple,"[1] by means of the interior illumination of the human spirit, as he describes in his *De Magistro* ("On the Teacher") in Augustinian categories. This does not mean intellectual softness or lack of rigor—the propositions are clear, the arguments carefully linked, and the product is concise and solid. Truth requires, in this spiritual charity, a tough-minded love.

THE CHURCH ON EARTH

At the same time that St. Thomas was examining these problems of faith and its witness in the world, another stream of thought was springing out of the new mendicant orders, expressing both the evangelical hopes of this apostolic Christian movement and the problematic institutional challenge that it raised. In October 1255, Pope Alexander IV condemned the *Introduction to the Eternal Gospel*. Gerard of San Donnino, a Franciscan teaching in Paris, wrote this text in order to present the ideas of Joachim of Flora who, sixty years earlier, had presented himself as the prophet of a new Christianity. The *Eternal Gospel* fits in at the end of two previous stages in the economy of salvation history as the coming of the age of the Holy Spirit. Uncovering the truths of the age of the Father (the Old Testament) and the age of the Son (the New Testament), the Spirit will soon inaugurate an age of love that will transcend institutional observances and formalities and serve as the prelude to the coming City of God.

Joachim of Flora (+ ca. 1205) was a monk from Calabria, a man of great culture with a reputation for sanctity. He had been influenced by the vision of the oriental Christian churches and he had adopted as his own the theme of several Greek doctors and spiritual theologians in the course of his evangelical awakening. They had reinterpreted the Platonic doctrine of an evolutionary emanation of the world as a way of describing God's plan revealed in the Scriptures. God, through an outpouring of divine love, enters into communion with humankind in the unfolding of history. In this evolutionary development, the progress of revelation is marked by a kind of earthly representation of the interior life of the Trinity of divine Persons.

[1] William of Tocco, *Vita Sancti Thomae Aquinatis,* op. cit., ch. 26, 99.

As early as the twelfth century, a conservative monk like Rupert of
Deutz or Anselm of Havelburg, a theologian sensitive to the Church's
transformation through history, in contrast to the cultural immobility
of Byzantine orthodoxy, had adopted the grand vision of Gregory
Nazianzus exalting the kingdom of the Father in the Old Testament,
the new alliance achieved in the incarnate Son, and the expansion of
the Spirit's rule little by little throughout the Church—all seen as a
reading of the testimony of the Scriptures.

Joachim of Flora had loaded on to this Greek theological tradition
even more ambiguities by prophesying the dissolution of the institutional aspects of the kingdom of God, and claiming that the eschatological future is calling us out of the present order of things. Using a
distorted allegorical interpretation, he saw the reign of the Father in
the Old Testament as only a provisional dispensation, while in the
New Testament, the incarnation of the Son was merely an episode
preparing for the Spirit's decisive coming. Within this trinitarian evo-
lutionism, the Church would simply disappear as institution and as
sacrament.

The evangelical revival at the end of the twelfth century seemed
to come exactly in time to give expression to this mystagogical
imagination—a new outpouring of the Spirit, allowing new apostles
who were announcing the end of an age to repudiate the blind mistakes of past generations and to liberate the Church from the burden
of its earthly institutions. All of this nurtured by its corrosive theological ideas the already evident tendencies of the evangelical sects.

Pope Innocent III somehow knew how to firmly hold on to the
truth of the Church, its magisterium, its institution of episcopacy, and
its sacraments while still taking advantage of the unquestionably valuable personal and ideological resources coming out of the apostolic
movements of both laity and clergy. Joachim of Flora remained in
communion with the pontiff. Francis of Assisi and Dominic the
Preacher, in spite of their differences, were both authentic heralds of
the presence of the Spirit in the Church.

The Franciscans and the Dominicans had been at the start very sensitive to this vision of a kingdom of God where the transcendent
power of the word of God and the progressive role of the Spirit would
together be made evident. However certain personalities, like Gerard
of San Donnino who articulated the Joachimite theory (with the sym-
pathetic encouragement of the Franciscan Minister General John of
Parma), completely upset some traditional values that Joachim had

upheld, including the typological sense of salvation history. Gerard favored the radical dissolution of the Church into the most disordered kind of spiritual anarchy.

Despite Gerard of San Donnino's eulogy of St. Francis as the prophet of the *Eternal Gospel* in his eschatological writings, the Friars Minor, with St. Bonaventure at their head, resisted such gross errors which, by the way, furnished the enemies of the mendicant orders with ammunition to denounce them. This the Masters of the University of Paris in fact did (incorrectly attributing the *Eternal Gospel* to a Dominican author); they called the mendicants "the peril of these last days." However, Pope Alexander IV categorically put a stop to these denunciations by confirming the evangelical and institutional validity of the Friars Minors and the Friars Preachers. Curiously, however, he failed to clearly condemn Joachim.

This time Thomas Aquinas would have to not only proclaim but theologically define the real integrity of the Church so described. It is noteworthy, first of all, that his theological teaching on the Church is not developed in a separate treatise. Rather, as with Bonaventure, Thomas's reflection on the Church both as institution and sacrament is developed within his theology of Christ and of the incarnation. The Church is the body of Christ, animated (given life) by the Spirit. Its organs are the apostolic institutions of various members under the leadership of the sovereign pontiff. At one and the same time, the Church is a body, a corporation in the sociological sense of the word, and the very mystery of Christ mystically and sacramentally extended in time and place.

The "biological" system of the Church (we might say) is the grace of the Spirit, this interior law that we have seen already put to striking use both in St. Thomas's theology and in the evangelical revival of the mendicants as well. The substance of the Church is constructed from the new life which faith, hope, and charity create in each believer. These are the virtues by which God is personally given to us as our object and destiny. Thus our communion in the Spirit can only be realized in community.

For St. Thomas, the Church is the entire apparatus of the creature's return to God, which he describes in the Second Part of the *Summa Theologiae*. And the Holy Spirit is the principle and the agent of this return, for Christian life is defined in terms of the human tendency toward the objects that represent God's very life. The Spirit is the soul of the Church.

The institutional Church is thereby the visible form of the Mystical Body of Christ. Its ministers are the sacrament of the Church. Its development through history maintains its essential identity, without denying the historical innovations which come over time to express its spiritual powers. In the light of the grandiose vision of the Church as a divine economy, taught by the Greek doctors, the incarnation of Christ and his visible social body spell out the historical and theological mediation of the Church, keeping its eschatological tendencies from turning it into a spiritual theocracy.

The very structure of St. Thomas's *Summa Theologiae,* built upon this conception of the return of the creature to its God by way of the historical reality of the incarnation, illustrates the balanced originality of this synthesis. This was a theological vision that neither the Reformers nor the Counter-Reformation could understand or respect. It is nothing less than sensational to recognize that the Masters of Theology of these evangelical generations, during a time of grave crisis in the history of Christianity and on the threshold of the beginning of modernity, were the ones to define the Church theologically—its christological nature, its spiritual constitution, its divinizing interiority, its hierarchical structure, and its infallibility as a witness to the gospel. The Church of the incarnation, in the succession of its historic manifestations of Christianity, is the embodiment and the norm of the Church of the Spirit.

THE NEW APOSTLES

The Masters of Paris were among the most vehement adversaries of the *Eternal Gospel.* Their delegate, William of Saint Amour, a man both able and intemperate, became their spokesperson at the papal court of Rome. The Parisian Masters accused the mendicants of being the organized expression of Joachimite mysticism. The Masters rejected not only the mendicants' influence as a spiritual movement, but also their apostolic initiatives and their theology. The Masters presented themselves as the defenders of the institutional establishment, protectors of the "foundations of the Church" (cf. the Manifesto of the University of Paris, February 1254) against the menacing subversion of these "new apostles." A good number of bishops who had only accepted mendicants in their dioceses under pressure from the Roman Pontiff, gave administrative and political support to these denunciations by the Parisian Masters in order to preserve the old-fashioned structures that provided them feudal security against the growing pressure of the communes and the guilds.

The Seal of the Faculty of Arts of the University of Paris, from A. Tulier, p. 247.

This was not merely a quarrel about precedence in the world of clerics; it expressed the critical competition between two tendencies at large in this moment of Christianity's evolution. Even the common people were divided, including the young students at the university; one part came thronging to the Friars Preachers and the Friars Minor, the other clung to the old forms in opposition to the new. The very existence of the two orders was questioned, both because of their apostolic orientation as well as their evangelical spirit. We have already seen how St. Thomas found the opportunity in Paris in 1256 to affirm his special vocation and to describe the power of the word of God in the world according to the Church's apostolic character.

So we should recognize in this local controversy over the mendicants' right to teach at the University of Paris, stirred up by William of Saint Amour, as well as in other protests against the mendicants and their usurpation of an apostolic mission, examples of a certain vision of what Christianity is all about. Underneath the rivalries of the different parties and their associated conflict of interests, there stands the paradoxical phenomenon that periodically arises in the Church and that is always disconcerting to the establishment, whether yesterday or today—the more that new ecclesial initiatives are spiritually and apostolically liberated, the more they become connected to the world, its economy, its culture, and its aspirations, touching not only the influential apparatus of the university, but other social forces as well. In any case, it is always true that the more theology is genuine theology, the more the rational disciplines of philosophy will manifest their coherence. Grace promotes the freedom of nature and encourages its rational methodology. At this very moment, Albertus Magnus and Thomas exercised their wits in contest with the Augustinian conservatism of the doctors in power.

William of Saint Amour, profiting from the ambiguities of the *Eternal Gospel,* and the bishops trading on the traditionalism of their pastoral roles, won the day, however. In 1254, Pope Innocent IV confirmed the decisions of the Masters of Paris and published a bull requiring a partial dissolution of the apostolic groups of the mendicant orders. But two weeks later, Innocent IV died, and his successor, Pope Alexander IV, immediately suspended the execution of the decrees of his predecessor. The condemnation of the *Eternal Gospel* purged the atmosphere of its doctrinal ambiguities, while the evangelical ideal of the Minors and the Preachers was publicly confirmed. The papal nomination of Thomas and Bonaventure to the title of Master of Theology was the dazzling finale to this episode.

Thomas and Bonaventure gave theoretical shape to the ecclesiology and spirituality of mendicant religious life. Fifteen years later, in the course of a new offensive, their theology and spiritual doctrine sufficed to legitimate the norms for religious life established outside of the structures of feudal monasticism. This time (in November 1269) St. Thomas responded to the same complaints and the same arguments laced with accusations against the "false preachers" not by responding point by point, but rather by composing an entire treatise. It treated Christian perfection and the state of perfection, the role of poverty, the legitimacy of the vows in the context of an apostolic life, the relative perfection of the various states of life (secular, religious, episcopal and pastoral)—all obliged and called in their diverse states of life to the same perfection of charity.

Thomas went well beyond the issues raised by the controversial accusing pamphlets when he treated of the juridical and spiritual structure of the Church and of its forms, "offices," and "states of life." Each of these is defined in an organized treatise whose enduring value surpasses the occasion that prompted its composition. (Cf. *Summa The-ologiae*, II–II, questions 179–89.) It is from these texts that we earlier borrowed the theology of the contemplative and the apostolic life—a theology nested inside an ecclesial organism that is both personal and collective, where the grace of the Holy Spirit is the very soul of the institution and the guarantee of its sacramental nature as well as the ultimate norm of its life of virtue.

TEXTS

Love or Action

There are three degrees of friendship. A friend can renounce delight in being in the beloved's presence in order to serve the beloved's needs: this is the perfection of friendship, since in friendship the beloved is loved for herself or himself and not for the delight that they give to their friend. On the contrary, the friend can take pleasure in the delight of being with the beloved to the point of preferring that to going off to serve; but then the beloved is loved only because of the pleasure he or she offers. On the other hand, if the friend easily forsakes the presence of the beloved so as to take interest in other things, then the friendship is only mediocre or empty.

The love of God is like this too, according to these three degrees, although God deserves to be loved more than anything else for God's own sake. Some willingly cease to give themselves to divine contemplation without much unhappiness in order to attend to earthly concerns: they have little or no love.

Others feel such delight in their contemplation of God that they refuse to give it up so as to serve God through the salvation of their sisters and brothers. But finally still others achieve such a fullness of love that they set aside the divine contemplation in which they take real delight in order to serve God in their sisters and brothers. This is the perfection we find in the Apostle Paul; it is the perfection that is expected of bishops and of preachers.

Quaestio disputata on Charity, q. 1, art. 11, resp. 6

Saint Thomas the Controversialist

There are actually people who presume that their judgment is so reliable that they can measure by their own understanding the nature of anything: they think that whatever they judge true is true, and whatever they judge false must be wrong.

Summa contra Gentiles, Bk. 1, ch. 5

In affirming or rejecting opinions, we shouldn't be influenced by our liking or dislike of those who propose the ideas, but rather by the certitude of truth. Aristotle says that we should love both those persons whose opinions we accept as well as those whose ideas we reject, since both types are applying themselves to the search for truth and, in that respect, both are collaborators with us in our own search. It goes without saying that we must follow the more certain, that is, the opinion which more clearly leads us to the truth.

Commentary on the Metaphysics, Bk. 12, lesson 9

If somebody chooses to write against my explanations, that is fine with me. There is simply no better way to discover the truth and to refute errors than to defend yourself against those who oppose your positions.

On the Perfection of the Christian Life, final section

Just as in the courtroom you can't make a judgment until you have heard both sides of a case; so also, if you are going to be a philosopher, you have to listen to all the thinkers with their opposing positions in order to have more resources for making a good judgment.

Commentary on the Metaphysics, Bk. 3, lesson 1

No one is more solicitous than Thomas Aquinas to leave open all the doors through which different minds can arrive in their own way at the same truth. No less committed than Duns Scotus to excluding errors, Thomas carefully cultivates the seeds of truth wherever he finds them. Every formulation, even one foreign to his way of thinking, receives from him an acknowledgement of partial truth to the degree this is possible. Thomas has the gift of uniting great suppleness with great firmness. You might first imagine that he bargains and judges in a spirit of compromise. But those who know him well are not fooled: he never grants the half-truth any other status than that of a step toward the fullness of truth.

E. Gilson, *Duns Scot* (Paris, 1952) 626

The Dialogue with Unbelievers

It is difficult to argue against errors. First of all, we know too little about the troubling ideas of different opponents, so we can't begin our argument (as we should) by examining what they really feel in order to critically rejoin their false conclusions. The doctors of early times knew the doctrines of the pagans, since they had once themselves been pagans (or had at least lived among them) and were acquainted with how they thought.

Further, we can't have recourse in dialogue with the Muslims or pagans to the same authorities to support our arguments. With the Jews, we can bring the Old Testament to bear; with heretics, the New Testament. But unbelievers do not accept these books. So with unbelievers we are obliged to have recourse to pure reasoning, to which everyone can give their assent. But reason is feeble in treating of divine matters.

In dealing with reasonable truths, we can convince our opponent through rational arguments; but in treating of God's revelation, our investigations have to go beyond the toil of reasoning. We should not seek to convince others concerning revelation by reasonable arguments, but reason only to resolve objections to the faith by showing that they do not contradict the faith.

The methodology of theological discussion implies the authority of God's word confirmed by miracles, since it is exclusively upon this word that we build our faith in the supernatural truths about God. In dialogue with believers, we can certainly have recourse to arguments of convenience (persuasion) to expand and strengthen their already existing faith. But we can't do this with unbelievers; otherwise the inadequacy of our rational arguments might confirm them in their denial of the faith and lead them to imagine that our own assent in faith is based upon only the poor reasoning we come up with.

Summa contra Gentiles, Bk. 1, ch. 2 and 9

The Holy Spirit, Soul of the Church

Each human being is a composite of body and soul, made up however of diverse members. The Catholic Church is also like this: it is one single body with many diverse members. The soul that gives life to this body is the Holy Spirit. That is why near the end of the Creed, after having professed our faith in the Holy Spirit, we add: and "the Holy Catholic Church."

The Church is the gathering up of believers into one holy Church of which each Christian is a member. . .

The Church is therefore *one.* There are three causes which produce this unity. First, there is unity of faith: all Christians who make up the body of the Church profess the same truth. Second, there is the unity of hope: all are straining toward the same hope of achieving eternal life. Third, there is the unity of love: all are linked together in the love of God and in a mutual love among themselves. If this love is authentic, it is expressed in an active concern of the members for one another and in a common sharing of one another's trials.

The Church is also *holy.* There are three sources of sanctity for the faithful who belong to the ecclesial body. First, they are sanctified by baptism. Just as a church building is materially purified to ready it for consecration, so also the faithful are washed in the Blood of Christ. Second, they are sanctified by anointing. Just as the church building is anointed, so are the faithful by a spiritual anointing that sanctifies them; otherwise they would not be called *Christians,* since Christ means *Anointed by God.* Third, they are sanctified by the indwelling of the Holy Trinity. . .

The Church is likewise *catholic,* meaning universal. First, this is true as to place, since the Church extends over the whole world. . . . Second, the Church is catholic with respect to the condition of its members: no one is excluded—neither prince nor servant; neither man nor woman. . . . Third, the Church is catholic with respect to time: it began at the time of Abel and will endure until the end of the world. . . .

The Church of God is sturdy. A house is called sturdy when it has a good foundation. Here the principal foundation of the Church is Christ, its secondary foundation is the apostles and their teaching; this is why the Church is called *apostolic.*

Commentary on the Creed, art. 9

The Supreme Pontiff's Role in Promulgating the Faith

A new expression of the Creed is needed as a defense against new errors that arise. This new expression of the Creed is the responsibility of the one who has the right to settle authoritatively what belongs to the faith; thus the faith becomes firm and held firmly by everyone. This comes under the authority of the Supreme Pontiff (pope), to whose judgment are referred the greatest and most difficult problems of the Church. The Lord said to Peter, whom he had constituted as

Supreme Pontiff, "I have prayed for you so that your faith shall not fail; and you, for your part, confirm your brothers" (Luke 22:32).

This is because there must be only one faith for the whole Church, as Paul says (1 Cor 1:10): "Have no factions among yourselves, but be in agreement in what you profess." This unity could not exist unless questions arising out of faith were resolved by the one who presides over the whole Church and whose decisions are followed firmly by the whole Church. This is why it is the Supreme Pontiff's exclusive right to publish a new expression of the Creed, as likewise to determine all other matters affecting the entire Church (such as the convoking of a general council).

Summa Theologiae, II–II, q. 1, art. 10

The decisions of a council that has made a judgment about the faith do not take away from a subsequent council the power to formulate a new expression of the Creed—which will contain not another faith, but the same faith more explicitly articulated. This is how the councils have acted, later ones amplifying the meaning of what earlier ones had said because of a need to clarify an issue raised by some heretical teaching.

Summa Theologiae, II–II, q. 1, art. 10, ad 2

Development of understanding takes place in two ways. First, there is growth on the part of the teacher who progresses in understanding (whether working alone or in company with others) over the passage of time. This is how progress comes about in the human sciences discovered by researchers. Second, there is growth on the part of students: a Master who knows the art of teaching doesn't try to impart his knowledge all at once to his student, who couldn't absorb it, but rather teaches little by little in a way accommodated to the student's capacities. This is the way that human beings have grown in their knowledge of divine faith throughout time [taught by their Divine Master]. This is why Paul (Gal 3:24) compares the time of the Old Testament to a period of childhood.

Summa Theologiae, II–II, q. 1, art. 7, ad 2

5: *Imago Mundi*

In 1267, Bonaventure, the colleague and friend of Thomas Aquinas who had become the Minister General of the Franciscans, gave a series of conferences traditionally offered to the students and Masters of the university during Lent. Following the *pro forma* requirement for a commentary of some sort on the Ten Commandments, Bonaventure addressed one of the most burning issues at that moment. About five years earlier, Aristotelian thought, though once censored by ecclesiastical decree, had gained the right to be included among official topics for instruction and had become firmly rooted as one of the enthusiasms of the Masters.

The wider circulation of the works of Averroes, the Aristotelian commentator *par excellence*, was forcing interpreters to give up mere pious accommodations of Aristotle in order to be more faithful to the text of the Stagirite. Until now, however, it had been Aristotle the logician, the master of the art of reasoning, who had been the focus of attention after a long period of resistance. But at this point, Aristotle's philosophy of nature and of human nature were considered even more appealing. Theologians were confronted not only with useful new methodologies (which they could integrate into their work), but also with independent new ideas about nature and anthropology that raised topics for serious reflection beyond the revealed data of the faith. Given this dualism of content and source, could the truth remain one?

Bonaventure, who was certainly not ignorant about the techniques and general principles of the Aristotelians, but who used them (in a pejorative sense of the term "use") within a worldview foreign to their spirit and tone, reacted forcefully against a full endorsement of authentic Aristotelianism and against the strong attraction that it was exercising in support of the growing autonomy of reason. As he had

From the vaulted ceiling of Cluny, the Agnus Dei—*the Lamb of God who conquered death, 11ᵗʰ or 12ᵗʰ cent. From the* Bourgogne Romane, *plate 39.*

done in similar cases, he concentrated on the problematic consequences of the system, more than on its principles. His judgment was strongly phrased: he condemned as errors of faith the propositions holding for the eternity of the world, the necessity of the natural law, and psychological determinism and the impersonal nature of human intelligence.

These were logical conclusions from the Aristotelian conception of the world that threatened the familiar articulations of Christian doctrine. The three propositions called into question a certain way of conceiving the theology of the human person in its personal and religious relation with God. Moreover, they resituated these questions outside of the framework of history and outside the revealed witness of the Scriptures.

In the following year, 1268, Bonaventure attacked Aristotelian ideas with even greater vigor. Controversies had become more widespread and more impassioned, especially in the Faculty of Arts, where the direct reading of the text of Aristotle had a strong influence. In the Faculty of Theology, unanimity in the commitment to defending the faith did not hide profound differences of positions with respect to theological systems. Bonaventure had discreetly made reference to those who, without giving in to error, nonetheless made room for it under the pretext of their rational methodology.

Thomas Aquinas was someone who was notorious for his option for Aristotelian principles, and he saw himself targeted by Bonaventure. He had just recently returned from Italy where he had taught for ten years, and he had taken up his chair again at the University of Paris at the beginning of the academic year 1268. In a series of public lectures (whose text is preserved in the disputed questions *De spiritualibus creaturis* ["About Spiritual Creatures"] and *De anima* ["About the Soul"]), he restated his analysis of the psychological structures of the human person at both the bodily and spiritual level, and he defended the validity of the naturalistic methodology of Aristotle as it applies to this area. At the same time, in distinction to Averroes, he defended in a strongly worded pamphlet the personalism that lies at the heart of Aristotelian anthropology.

In the course of the solemn assemblies of Advent and Lent in which the current problems of the times were reviewed, Thomas defended the consubstantial unity of human body and soul with all the psychological and epistemological consequences that follow, in contrast to the idealist position of the Augustinians. It was doubtless at one of

Silhouette of St. Thomas, already haloed, from a 13ᵗʰ-century manuscript of his Commentary on Matthew.

these gatherings that Thomas in 1270 suffered the severe attack leveled by John Peckham, a Master of the rival school, fiercely accusing him of contaminating philosophy with naturalism. This event took place before the whole university in the presence of Master Stephen Tempier who had become the bishop of Paris. At the end of July, in a religious conference, Thomas distanced himself from the Averroist Siger de Brabant and made his famous statement about philosophers: they know less about the religious destiny of the human person than a simple old person who has naive but certain faith.

Nonetheless, lists of suspect propositions targeting Thomas Aquinas continued to circulate along with the threat of his condemnation. One of his Dominican brothers, disturbed by all this, sent a message to Albertus Magnus (if indeed this is the episode in question): he sought Albert's help, since Albert still had great prestige in Paris. The old Master, who did not completely share all the Aristotelian convictions of his former student, nonetheless vigorously took on the "sophist" theologians in Paris.

But the matter had gone too far. At the end of 1270, thirteen propositions summarizing the Averroist interpretation of Aristotle were denounced as irreconcilable with Christian faith; these included the eternity of the world, the denial of Providence, the denial of the spiritual personality of humans, and the denial of free will. At the last minute, two propositions which touched upon Thomas's teaching were withdrawn. Still condemned, however, was the thesis that the world might be eternal.

Thomas fearlessly objected in support of the idea of the eternity of the world, not in order to link himself in doctrinaire fashion with Aristotle as the Averroists did, but rather so as to be able to maintain the freedom of research (within the limits of the rule of faith). He reacted against the closed-minded conservatism of his opponents who refused completely to work through the ambiguities of the promising ideas of Aristotle.

Thomas Aquinas had to leave Paris the following year to take a chair in theology at the University of Naples. The Masters of Arts (today we would call them the professors of the Faculties of Arts and Sciences), whose philosophical methods Thomas had defended against the Augustinian supernaturalism of Bonaventure, publicly manifested their esteem and their thanks to their theologian friend to the point of further compromising him. In 1273, Bonaventure again took up the battle in a series of conferences in the style of a commentary on the biblical account of creation that clearly addressed the issues under debate. Bonaventure denounced the naturalistic foundations of a conception of the universe and of an anthropology that failed to support the Augustinian vision that he considered the criterion of authentic faith.

CREATURES ENCOUNTERING THE DIVINE ABSOLUTE

If I have given more space here to biographical details than elsewhere, it is first of all in order to break out of a kind of devotional imagery about the life of St. Thomas in which he is presented as an abstract and solitary personality insulated from the rough and tumble conflict of his century by his contemplative spirit and his occupation as a scholar. In this century of *Summas* and cathedrals, this century when Louis IX was both king and saint, we don't take seriously enough—outside of a simplistically romantic idea of the medieval—its brutal realities, where spiritual violence, even among believers, intensified the toughness of people's manners. Neither historical truth nor the personal magnanimity of St. Thomas allow for a soft and sentimental reading of his life.

These events that touch the core of Thomas's doctrinal career and the heart of his spirituality actually provide us with clues about the most significant crisis of ideas in the whole of the Christian world at this time. It is a shame that the Reformation and the Renaissance have almost completely hidden the significance for us of his role in these questions. In the genesis of modernity, Thomas undoubtedly provides the key (even for the Reformation and the Renaissance) to the problems raised about anthropology and grace, even taking into account the great multiplicity of theologies and spiritualities that develop after his death. Thomas Aquinas is the spiritual master of a conception of grace and nature in which their mutual involvement immediately illuminates their meaning, while still safeguarding their real distinction. Further, we highlight these currents of thought not for reasons of historical erudition, but because of the objective importance of Thomas's vision across historical perspectives, a vision that is still valid well beyond considerations of medieval scholastic disputations.

Is it possible that the world has existed from all eternity? Even though they may appear to be gratuitous, such questions about the origin and genesis of things have great importance. Through their technical formulation, they effectively shape the worldview and philosophical tendencies by which these issues are treated. Aristotle had built his theory of the universe upon principles that implied the eternity of the world. His analysis of essences never led him to search for a beginning for existence. The new fact that there was a "creation" did not enter into his perspective of a metaphysics of motion, within which a God intervening in time was inconceivable.

For believers reading the first chapter of the book of Genesis, however, there was here at least a contradiction of fact: the world *was* created. For Augustinian theologians, the idea of the eternity of the universe was a negation of the radical contingency of the creature; for them, given God's creative causality, this idea emptied the mystery of the dependency upon God which lies at the heart of all spirituality and which establishes the human being's title to being in the image of God. At the same time creation provides the reason for human submission to divine Providence.

How could St. Thomas support the possibility of an eternal creation, then? How could he uphold this idea to the point of endangering his reputation and his teaching? The answer is that for him the fact of a beginning of the world in time, as taught by Scripture, cannot fore-close the rational analysis of created being which properly belongs to a metaphysics of motion. The believer should "believe" in creation in time; the philosopher, however, must uphold the truth of his principles without contradicting his faith.

The relation of dependency upon God that is the foundation of all religion (and principally of interior religion) is not established upon some change, upon some contingent events in time, but rather upon a necessary ontological relation intrinsic to being itself, beyond any consideration of temporality. The scholar must have complete methodological freedom to explore the question of the world's genesis according to scientific principles.

Conversion to God is the intrinsic law of the relation of creature to Creator. Here we are at the depths of St. Thomas's vision, in reaction against an idea of "religion" that is still very much alive. In the Augustinian vision of the universe, the stress lies upon the dependency of being with respect to the relationship which constitutes it as creature: the admission of our ontological poverty is the expression of our "nothingness." For St. Thomas, creation still expresses this dependency of created being upon its very Source of existence (without which it would cease to exist). Further, our prayer is governed by this radical dependency. But the indomitable originality of this unique relationship must be carefully safeguarded against the perversions of a religiosity that would water it down.

It is essential to note first off that this relation is unilateral: God makes no contract in producing this emanation from divine Being—and cannot contract a real relation with a creature. God's transcendence excludes all change within the divine; it is unthinkable that even the production of these new creatures should add anything to God's Being. God's generosity is absolute. So the exchanges in this unimaginable communion happen through a doubly mysterious intimacy—as if in silence—something inconceivable in the dialogue of human partners face to face. This is not a case of an accidental shift in perspective within a hierarchy of objects where God is the divine Super-Object with just a higher degree of reality than the human spirit. No, God is not grasped by any category of any science or any philosophy. Says John's Gospel: "No one has ever seen God." And St. Thomas adds in the *Summa Theologiae* I, q. 3: "We are not able to know what God is, but only what God is not, and what relation everything else has to God."

The second and no less decisive element of the creature's condition is this: when creation came about, at the heart of the being that it receives from God is placed an ontological link—a pure relation where the poverty of the created one is expressed—and the creature is thus bound to God even as it is set forth in existence. To be created is first of all to *be*: the being is of one who is dependent, always linked to its source of being, but whose dependence only has significance because it is something that *is*. This fact has real priority in the order of being: what is created *is* by reason of its relation to its Creator.

This is the foundation for the realism expressed in the hierarchy of natures and in the interplay of secondary causality. At the very core of creation and of the radical dependency that affects every finite being, authentic autonomy will come into play. Even within their ontological poverty and consistent with their character as finite spirit, human creatures still come to exercise a real personal autonomy (an idea that Augustinian thought refused to accept because of its reaction to Greek thought).

The very immanence of Providence—which is not at all an abstract order in the universe but a continuing creation—defines the dependency of every created thing in relation to creative Wisdom. Providence guarantees here again within the Creator-creature relationship the reality of the order of natures. From this relationship flow their appropriate actions. God's sovereign power actualizes every created thing. But this sovereign governance which God exercises over the universe stays within the laws of creative Providence, which seeks from each created being activities in conformity with its nature that emerge from it as its own.

This autonomy finds its highest realization in human rationality, that moves itself both in its intellectual endeavors as well as in its moral choices. Its liberty, far from being alienated by its relation to God, finds its foundation in that relation. God is God and not a projection of earthly powers. Providence is not a gracious supplement given to help us through our incapacities at precarious moments. Providence is the act through which we receive everything necessary to achieve our destiny. This is the very meaning of our being "in the image and likeness of God," to be able to exercise this creative freedom. But every creature likewise comes forth from God into its being and its activity, and with a genuinely real reality. The presence of God is the consecration of this fundamental reality of the real.

When Augustine talks about the things and events of this world as being permanently present to God who knows them, he is thinking only about their eternal presence as "ideas" in the divine Mind. So within this system of thought that Nietzsche would contemptuously call "Christianity as Platonism for the people," the historic economy of grace and nature in mutual interaction is incomprehensible except in terms of haphazard events. The economy of grace as Augustine saw it (considered unchangeable) was constructed beyond our understanding in a world of ideas situated in God.

For his part, St. Thomas established the idea of a divine foreknowing by way of the concept of the coexistence of God at each moment within the flux of time. Things *are* and temporal events *are*—not just their "eternal reasons." The theocratic theology of the Augustinian position considered ideas as the locus of truth and counterposed them to passing existences, making ideas the object of a fallacious science that is relegated to subservience to religiosity. But in Thomism, "temporal becoming is absolutely real; God's creative grasp gives consistency to duration in time where it becomes the principle of life, of consciousness, and of freedom."[1] The Logos of God is not a Platonic divinity.

Within this religious metaphysics—where the real distinction between essence and existence is the key theoretical problem—within this ontological optimism, things have their consistency; and among created things human beings have this consistency within their freedom. Natures have their dependable structure, as we have already said with reference to the creative wisdom of God. But divine wisdom is expressed and perceptible precisely in its coming to realization. The world has an order which derives not from arbitrary omnipotent divine decisions, but from the actual structure of created being just as it has proceeded from its divinely ordered plan.

In a sense, God is obliged to respect creation since divine wisdom is at issue; this is a matter of divine justice (which is one of the attributes of God's provident will). To know the will of God, we don't have to escape the world to seek (by what possible paths?) the secret of a supremely arbitrary spirit. There is no other path to God except to examine the realities of nature in order to discern the subtle signs of

---

[1] A. Hayen, "Le 'cercle' de la connaissance humaine selon saint Thomas d'Aquin," *Revue philosophique de Louvain* 54 (1956) 589.

God's wisdom and then, in the light of faith, to discover in sacred history the promises and the assurance of a coherent plan of salvation.

Yet for Bonaventure, it was dangerous to attribute too much to creatures, and humility should be inclined (even at the cost of truth) to minimize their role. For Thomas Aquinas, to give created beings their due was to give fuller glory to God, since the capacity with which creatures are endowed is precisely the super-effect of an astonishing divine omnipotence. *To diminish the perfection of creatures, is to diminish the perfection of the divine power.*[2] This is even more the case with respect to those free beings who are human. God is equally the source and master of such differences in their being as contingency and necessity, determinism and freedom, conferring on each their special quality: "To dispense himself from their government, God would have to dispense himself from giving them being."[3]

In the world's destiny, God's role is not that of the helper of human beings within a shared partnership in which God would provide power and courage along with some assurance of eternal happiness. God controls history, precisely because events *are totally human* within this creative providence. The very transcendence of God is the reason for the real efficacy of nature, of causes, and of events—for "the will of God, if we understand that it is beyond the order of things, is the cause penetrating the depths of being in its totality, all distinctions included."[4] The natural law is not the projection of timeless decrees into the heart of history, as Scotus thought, but rather a concrete commandment of God that enters into the very details of a situation. This is not relativism: because of its divine origin, the natural law has the capacity to guide our societies through their tumultuous events.[5]

This realism is not at all the result of a latent naturalism, as pietistic idealism always accuses it. Pietism is only satisfied by Platonic religious values. St. Thomas continually challenged the Platonic worldview with its dualism of matter and spirit, its split into two of human intelligence, its too easy contempt for sensible things, and its

[2] *Summa contra Gentiles*, Book 3, ch. 69.

[3] Ibid., Book 3, ch. 1.

[4] Aquinas's Commentary on the *Peri Hermeneias* of Aristotle, Book 1, Lesson 14, No. 197 (Turin, Marietti, 1955).

[5] A. Hayen, "Deux théologiens: Duns Scot et saint Thomas," *Revue philosophique de Louvain* 51 (1953) 233–94.

seduction by spiritual escapism. These are not the pathways of God and of the Bible.

"In the Platonic world, there is a need for evasion, an obligation to flee from certain things which are considered in themselves as irreconcilable with human hope. But we must notice that this supposed human obligation to flee effectively implies divine imperfection. The world of the patriarchs and the prophets, which is also a gospel world, is not a world where an obligation to flee because of human failure diminishes the divine plan. The God who 'in the beginning created the heavens and the earth' is according to Christian faith a God whose transcendence assures to everything that exists a 'goodness' through means of which God will always open a passage toward hope."[6]

It is admittedly paradoxical for Christian sensibilities that Aquinas had recourse to a philosophy that does not make the Transcendent its object. But in fact Thomas's decision to use Aristotle in his theological work was at the service of the historic realism and the earthly reality of the gospel message in which the incarnation is our route of access to intimacy with God.

In contrast to the mental and spiritual evasions of a sort of providentialism and in contrast to ecstatic transcendentalism, the true means for entering into God's plan is to become attached to the knowledge of secondary causes to the degree that we can know them. We need to follow their lead along the ontological and epistemological levels of earthly realities, adopting the appropriate method for each different reality, both within natural science as well as within historical studies.

The same is true with regard to the moral law, which is discovered and defined by examining human nature, not by setting out with *a priori* ideas about the eternal law (which is the source of all genuine morality). This is also true for the dynamics of human freedom, where the causality of reason over free will is made manifest through the power of objects, which are not merely simple occasions (as the Augustinians held from an obsessive fear of determinism), but intrinsic and efficacious causes of human choice. The same is true in all the areas of human thought and action within the Christian economy of

[6] J.-P. Audet, "Le sacré et le profane, leur situation dans le christianisme," *Nouvelle revue théologique* (1957) 53.

"St. Thomas Aquinas Confounding Averroes," by
Giovanni de Paolo, The St. Louis Art Museum.

salvation. In each order of reality, problems are posed and solutions
are found through the means of the appropriate objects and according to the appropriate methods.

The Averroist thinker Boethius of Dacia, who was implicated in the
condemnation of 1270 along with St. Thomas, wrote the following:
"No specialist can demonstrate, recognize, or reject a proposition except in virtue of its principles, that is, the principles of its appropriate
science." So you can't resolve a political problem with religious reasons or an economic problem with moral argumentation. Albertus
Magnus had already expressed that in the philosophy of nature, he
preferred Aristotle to Augustine—using each of them according to his
competence. St. Thomas said the same: "The judgment that bears on a
reality or on an action must be taken from their proper principles."[7]

---

[7] *Summa Theologiae*, I–II, q. 57, art. 6, resp. 3.

That is the old methodological axiom that Boethius—the master thinker for the Aristotelians—formulated in these terms: a spiritual being that is its own master treats each thing according to the way it is in itself.

Here is undoubtedly the principal trait not only of St. Thomas's epistemology, but also of his religious spirit. Today, as in St. Thomas's time, it is the bad will of his adversaries that leads them to fragment the truth into disjointed and separated levels. Yet in contrast to persistent confusion, pious opportunism, and every kind of voluntarism, Thomism—faithful to objects—remains constant in its vocation "to distinguish in order to unite" (to use the phrase of Jacques Maritain).

THE HUMAN PERSON AND MATTER

This intellectual methodology when applied to the human subject becomes pregnant with a spirituality insightful about the fundamental condition of human nature. Here Thomas Aquinas and his contemporaries stand at a point of even more decisive disagreement. Certainly all teach that the human person is both soul and body, or, following philosophical terms, spirit and matter. But this agreement common to both faith and reason leaves the field open to rival expressions not only of biblical terms and philosophical categories, but also of rival analyses of the structure and function of matter and spirit. The way we imagine the reality will clearly shape the outcome of differing anthropologies and spiritualities.

Giving in to the pressure of a latent Platonism transmitted by the philosophy of Augustine, theologians and spiritual writers tend to think of the union of soul and body only as the precondition of an independent substantial soul. The soul's union with matter is thought to affect it only accidentally. Although the human spirit achieves its present and future destiny in a body, this body is considered to be little more than the temporal envelope of a life destined to escape the blemish of time. A kind of spiritual imperialism arises out of this attitude which holds itself above the degradation of centrifugal bodily energies, as well as above the contamination of the world of matter with which the human body as body is in solidarity. The genius of Augustine overcame many of the harmful illusions of this kind of spirituality. But the system built upon his thought, called Augustinianism, held firmly in place all the consequences implicit in these ideas.

St. Thomas himself explicitly refused not only the consequences but also the principles of this Augustinian anthropology. Was this because he was a disciple of Aristotle, whose controversy with Plato was being revived in the thirteenth century? It seems clear that Thomas's position was formed not only in the midst of scholastic disputes, but also at the living center of his own personality. If he comments upon Aristotle, the reason is that he perceives in Aristotle the means to ground himself in reason and in sound methodology in order to be able to construct a system. Neither the system nor the controversial interpretation of Aristotle controls his theological vision—a vision already emerging when he took notes in the courses of his Master Albertus Magnus.

By contrast with any dualistic understanding, Thomas sees the human person as constituted as one single being where matter and spirit by their mutual inherence are consubstantial principles of one determined totality without any gap: the person is not two things, not a soul having a body or moving a body, but an incarnated soul, an animated body, in such fashion that the soul is determined as the "form" of the body. This affects the most intimate reality of the person to such a point that without the body it would be impossible to have awareness of its own being. "For the body to have a soul is the same thing as for the matter of this body to be rendered actual."[8]

A chemical compound is a unity whose radicals are something utterly different, once they are brought together into this new unity; the radical elements are no longer independent substances. Even more is the unity of matter and spirit in the human composite decisively one. Spirit and matter allow each other to exist; they mutually constitute, sustain, and determine one another. By reason of this consubstantiality, matter within the human person is able to participate in divine life and, through the gracious gift of the life of Christ the Man-God, the Risen One is the guarantee of a resurrection of glorified flesh. The human person is the agent of the expansion of creative love into the very texture of matter.

They failed to remember that they are humans.[9] This saying of Thomas is telling not only as applied to the Cathars (meaning the "pure ones"), but as applied to anyone who imagines *purity* of spirit—in its being, its works of knowledge and love, its act of contemplation, and its destiny—as only a progressive alienation from the

---

[8] See Aquinas's Commentary on Aristotle's *De anima*, Book 2, lesson 1, ending (Turin: Marietti, 1948).

[9] *Summa contra Gentiles*, Book 3, ch. 119.

body and from social constraints. *If the body weighs down the soul,* replies St. Thomas, *it is not because of the nature of the body, but because the body is becoming corrupt.*[10] Neither the immortality of the soul, nor contemplation, nor the "interior life," nor the absolute dignity of the human person, nor human freedom is threatened by this *natural* unity of body and soul. Within the human composite, the spirit remains the subject (recipient) of being and the principle of subsistence. It has an ontological primacy which establishes in human nature not only the spirit's mastery and its taste for the divine objects that lift it up, but also the spiritual combat against the "flesh," the *contemptus mundi* found in the gospel.

It follows that the "interior life," beginning with self-knowledge, develops not by way of avoiding things—human freedom is not a refuge from external or psychological determinisms, and the person is not forced to avoid social contacts in order to be spiritual. This eliminates the mentality (more or less explicit) that thinks that humans use their bodies only as a provisional organ—a mediating instrument—thanks to which the person lifts itself above the disturbing images of the material world into a realm of pure essences that are absolute and detached from matter. Such escapist spirituality imagines that it reaches into an ideal domain that is universal, without any trace of the material, where it can already find the eternal, changeless place natural to the spirit. Here it imagines itself in a prelude to that rest which will finally surmount the burden of this earthly life, a life unworthy of a spiritual nature.

Albertus Magnus, although strongly attracted to the biological empiricism of Aristotle, nonetheless resisted a realist spirituality. With others he distinguished between several "forms" within the unity of the soul. These different levels supposedly assured the independence of the spirit in its interaction with the spiritual world, isolating it from the body's involvements with the world here below. His philosophical analysis was similar to the teaching of the majority of spiritual masters (at Cîteaux in particular) who distinguished a faculty for knowing the divine, at the summit of the soul, that was detached from the intellect which is enslaved to the body. That higher "form" was a place of supreme purity where one could experience the presence of God.

---

[10] *Quaestiones disputatae De potentia*, q. 3, art. 10, resp. 17.

St. Thomas reacted strongly against this compromise which allowed for the continued influence of Platonic and Augustinian dualism. Thomas insisted that there is only one substantial "form" in the human being. The exact same form that directs the actions of the spirit is the one that achieves the physical and organic information of the body. There is only one intelligence which both contemplates God and knows the world. There are not two aspects of the human soul, one turned toward the eternal and the other attached to temporal duties. There is not, on the one hand, "reason" characterized as searching, inquiring, discursive, and bound to concepts and to imagery and, on the other hand, an "intellect" characterized as gradually liberated from the weight of analyses, reasoning, and mental constructions. No, the spirit of the human person is one and the same. From the organic ensoulment of the body to the vision of divine realities, the same spirit rules over the interplay of the passions and also becomes through grace the dwelling place of the Holy Spirit.

Despite the condemnation that Bishop Stephen Tempier would pronounce in his famous syllabus of 1277, this position would be firmly maintained by the first disciples of St. Thomas. It is the inflexible criterion of his spirituality and at the very heart of his understanding of the human person. So a vision faithful to Thomas, without prejudicing functional differentiations within the person or the soul as substantial form, will always try to establish a unity within all the analyses and all the categories that philosophers and spiritual writers propose from the accounts of their experiences.

Bit by bit, through the ups and downs of philosophy and theology, the disciples of St. Thomas drew the consequences of this unity of the human person in the face of doctrines as different as Manichaeism and Cartesianism. This unity is the root of our insertion in nature, beginning with humanity's fleshly condition. The most immediate consequence of this doctrine is the refusal to separate intellectual life and spirituality—a schism that is ruinous both for the intellect and for the human spirit. Applied to the understanding of the Christian mysteries, this radical coherence of matter and spirit became the very foundation for a theology in which the powers of reason develop under the guidance of faith into a full and valid homogeneity in the light of the divine Spirit.

As we said in chapter two, the spirituality of St. Thomas is in fact really intrinsic to his theology. His trust in human intelligence is the effect and the guarantee of a sense of mystery. In Thomism, according to the well-known expression of Père Gardeil, the intellectual keeps its eye on the spiritual.

THE MORAL LIFE

Thomas's anthropology creates a structure which controls and defines in advance both the situation of the human person in the universe and the dynamics of human nature. Or better, the situation of human life in the universe (as the unifying link between spirit and matter) along with the intrinsic human tendency toward the perfection of its being, are the two coordinates of one same ontological condition. In any given instance of human intelligence and freedom, human nature provides the regulating direction, the initiatives, the development, the perfection, and the happiness within the order of nature. These are not exceptional expressions of life in the context of an altogether different spiritual world.

The dignity of moral life ought to be expressed in a consciousness aware of itself and its role, aware of the goods that it experiences, and aware of its love for the Supreme Good—the highest expression of the natural law (which does not diminish its subordination to the universe). The human person realizes its complete perfection and happiness with the full integrity of its being under the guidance of Providence. Isn't the deepest expression of God's liberality that God extends to creatures not only manifold participation in being, but the ability to be causes in their turn within the various levels of the hierarchical order of the universe?

In this way, each substance realizes its true end according to its own nature within the general goal-orientation of the universe. "Morality" becomes part of the "physical" order of the cosmos. For, at the top of creation, the spiritual creature—a singular phenomenon within the ensemble of natural beings—will be both submissive to divine Providence, on the one hand, and to the providential principle of its own acts, on the other. Human freedom is rooted in nature, and the natural law is equipped with the imperative of a free will.

The person—an absolute value by reason of this freedom—will always be nonetheless part of a greater whole. Its self-love needs to develop through loving others, for to love oneself truly is to choose to be in one's just place in the order of things. The love of God found within the depths of things is the unifying reason for my attachment to my own self and for my love of others. *If then the goodness, the beauty, and the sweetness of creatures attract the human soul, this is be-*

cause the living source of divine Goodness, expressed in each creature as in so many little streams and carefully captured there, attracts completely to itself fully human souls inflamed with its charms.[11]

In this spirit Thomas opens up the Second Part of the *Summa Theologiae*, commonly considered the moral teaching of his theology. Unquestionably there are surprises here for a certain type of moralist who looks only at *a priori* considerations and who extrapolates metaphysical and mystical ideas foreign to practical human behavior and to its internal criteria of freedom. St. Thomas, by contrast, finds that moral science is theological—and simultaneously both theoretical and practical. The goal of moral science is to see and to situate all beings (and being itself) in proper relation to God from whom they all emerge within a well-defined participation which leads them back to God.

Happiness, virtues, laws, asceticism, moral behavior—all these are of course the topics for a discipline responsible for directing human action. But this discipline will only attain theological understanding of its object—the human person in the universe—by seeing it in the light of the creative act. By God's initiative the human creature not only exists, but—by the same divine action—reaches toward and organizes its own existence so as to continue and to complete its procession out from God, its Source.

Moreover, if the creature is set in being and in action with the resources of its nature by the very act of the creative Cause, as we have seen, then the "return" back to God will find its direction and its norms in the right functioning of this nature that is the rule of its own perfection and happiness. In the privileged case of human beings, spiritual creatures achieve their return to God with a free, personal conscience, with no need of cosmic mediation. But this free, spiritual self-mastery in no way removes the "morality" of this law by which every created nature develops and reaches its ultimate destiny within the cosmic movement of procession and return. If we were to consider God's action as no more than a simple assistance to human freedom, we would cut freedom at the root in the expression of even its most ephemeral intentions—just as we would turn moral conduct away from its *natural* rule if we were to connect it directly to the obligations of a divine imperative.

[11] *Summa contra Gentiles*, Book 2, ch. 2.

This conception of a human morality rooted in the natural and historical order of the world was developed and presented by St. Thomas on the basis of two fundamental doctrines. The first is borrowed from the grandiose Neoplatonic vision of the universe, conceived (humanity included) in terms of an emanation and a return inside a single movement that defines the dynamics of the creature's participation in divine Being. Thomas uses this schema to design the structure for his *Summa Theologiae*, within which salvation history, the incarnation of Christ included, enters into this predestined plan of divine Love's expansion. This formula was taken from the Greek Fathers, only recently rediscovered in Thomas's day. They purged the idea of emanation of its pantheism and its initial determinism, but they maintained beyond the context of historic Platonism this fascinating dialectic.

The second doctrine on which Thomas's moral vision rested was the biblical teaching that the human person was made "to the image and likeness of God" (Gen 2). Through its use of the idea of the image of God, the analysis of morality in the *Secunda Pars* is connected to the procession of creatures. Here is a new example of the insertion of moral issues within a theological vision and methodology. Once more, spirituality, substantially nurtured by the theme of the image of God, flows out of theology.

"In the theologian's understanding, to be human—that is to say intelligent, endowed with free will, master of oneself and one's acts—is to be the image of God. To become human, act human, or (if you prefer) to flow back toward God following the human mode and the characteristic resources available to humans through the creative flux—all this is literally to exercise one's role as image of God. By the same stroke, to the astonishment of the simple moralist, one thus treats God not as legislator, remunerator, or helper, or whatever else you want to call him, but as model."[12]

For the historian, isn't the thirteenth century the perfect secular realization of this high theological vision? The Gothic period is drawn more and more daringly into a spirituality of the *incarnation*, rather than of the *sacred* that was so characteristic of the Carolingian and the Romanesque. Here is a growing affirmation of the human, and through the human of the world. From an idealist universe, we pass

[12] Jean Tonneau, "Morale et théologie" in *Initiation théologique*, op. cit., vol. 3, 13–36.

into a universe where nature, history, and human action have more and more significance, becoming as vivacious and realistic as a narrative about ordinary life.

Here is the birthplace of secular art. *The Mirror of the World*, the encyclopaedia of Vincent of Beauvais, who was a contemporary and Dominican confrere of St. Thomas as well as the counselor and librarian of King St. Louis IX, is a very significant expression of this vision in its major interests: nature, human thought, morals, and history.

Neither nature, nor history, nor human achievements for all their vigor cease being religious. Observe the developments in both landscape and portrait painting. Nature and human beings find a place for themselves for their own sake, no longer merely as symbols. The folds of garments and the gestures of personalities cease being hieratic and become ordinary. Trees, fields, and rivers are portrayed with a palpable existence as concrete and solid—and along with these, so also the

Pillars of the transept of the Church of Paray le Monial, 12ᵗʰ cent. From the Bourgogne Romane, *plate 50.*

work of men and women. Their naturalistic realism and their secular social life apparently disconnect them from sacral significance; but then, in a stroke, they enter within the concrete unfolding of Providence and into the economy of an incarnate God. Abundant examples from the arts show us this incarnational spirituality:

- the whole of nature, from its flora and fauna down to the shape of the human body, from the impulses of love to the gestures of social life;
- William of Aquitaine's poetry about springtime, and the sensuous Eve sculpted at the cathedral of Autun;
- the drawings in the notebooks of Villard de Honnecourt, and the casuistry of love of Chrétien de Troyes;
- the sculptures of the crafts carved into the stone capitals of cloister gardens, and the taste for realism about human destiny in the works of the great chroniclers;
- the political psychology of John of Salisbury, and the anticlericalism of the second *Roman de la Rose*;
- the reduction of the rights of the clergy in secular matters undertaken by Philip Augustus or St. Louis IX, and the recourse to reasonable proofs in judgments of justice rather than to mystical means such as the ordeal, etc.

An entire "super-natural" world which had projected its image upon things and upon human hearts within Romanesque art as well as within early medieval social customs now became blurred in people's imaginations. Now that nature had been discovered in its secular reality, it would express its own religious values and lead people to God along quite different pathways. As to grace, it will possess in the eyes of artists as much power of conviction and emotion as nature itself.

TEXTS

A World Both One and Diverse

The diversity among things is not the result of chance, but an element making up a universe which requires variety. We must realize that the diversity and multiplicity among beings belong to the plan of the

Creator. If God brought things into existence, it was so that his goodness would be communicated to creatures and symbolized or represented through them. However, God can't be satisfactorily represented by one single creature, and so God produced many diverse creatures so that what was lacking in one expression of divine goodness could be supplied for by another. The Goodness which exists in God in simplicity and uniformity becomes in creatures multiple and scattered. So the universe as a whole reveals a more perfect participation in and representation of divine Goodness than any one creature possibly could. This is how God's wisdom decided that the world should be.

Summa Theologiae I, q. 47, art. 1

The Laws of Nature and of Grace in the Governance of the World

In the outpouring of creatures coming forth from their first principle, there is a sort of rotation or circulation from the fact that all beings moving toward their ultimate goal return to the source from which they came forth. So we observe that the same structure exists in their return as in their coming forth.

Now we have said that the production of creatures has as its final purpose the movement of persons back into divine Life: the same emanation [that produces a being] must be the highest principle for that being's return toward its final goal. Just as we have been created through the Son and the Spirit, so will we be in communion with our final goal through them.

The procession of the divine persons in creatures can be thought about in two ways. First, from the point of view of their coming out from God—and here the procession is understood in terms of the gifts of nature in which we subsist (stand forth in existence). The wisdom and the goodness of God are poured out into creatures, says Denis. But this procession can be thought of as well in terms of our return to the ultimate end of our lives, and this is brought about through the gifts which alone can unite us to our ultimate end. These are sanctifying grace and glory.

Commentary on the Sentences Book 1, dist. 14, q. 2, art. 2

The Communion of Beings and the Divine Peace of the Universe

Thanks to the Divinity, souls, by joining together the variety of their minds . . . are raised up by the method and the order appropriate for each one . . . all the way to the One (who surpasses all human understanding).

Perfect Peace spreads its plenitude across the whole spectrum of beings, thanks to the perfectly simple and unmixed immanence of God's uniting power . . . God makes all participate in divine delights, out to the furthest limits of the universe. . . . This Peace pours itself out everywhere and communicates itself to everything according to the mode that is appropriate to each, overflowing from the superabundance of its pacifying fertility.

Denis, The Divine Names, ch. 2

Divine peace establishes all things in an unconfused connection within a shared existence. There is nothing in creatures that does not have some kind of link or relation with all other creatures, whether as species or genus or some other order of relation. Yet none of them loses their unique properties . . . . In this perfect coherence, each being preserves the purity of its own species life. For this reason, the union of beings in no way confuses the autonomy of each, nor their intelligibility or powers . . . . The strength of each is in no way diminished . . . .

This is how we should think about this one and simple Nature which, by establishing unity, brings peace to reign over everything: it is the divine Nature which joins all things to Itself. It makes things like to itself by giving Its gifts, and It orders things to return to Itself as their final end or completion. In this way, the divine Nature unifies all things in themselves, that is to say, unifies each thing in itself. So finally each thing is unified with itself and with others in such fashion as to be in accord with each other.

The divine Nature upholds all things in an order of unity without confusion, so that all are harmonized in a concrete order, each thing maintaining its own specific purity of being even while expressing reciprocal relations of interaction with other beings.

Commentary on the Divine Names ch. 2, lesson 2

The Progress of the Spirit through History

Time is like an inventor, or perhaps a good partner. Not of course because time does anything by itself, but because the passage of time affects the results of our discoveries. If someone is committed over a long period of time to the search for truth, he or she will be helped by the passage of time in their efforts, either because they slowly discover things they had not known before or because they are assisted by what others have learned before them and so can move forward from there.

This is how the sciences make progress. From some modest initial finding, scholars move little by little toward the discovery of great masses of information. Each individual can add something that was lacking in the analysis of those who went before.

However, if the learning of the ages is not cultivated by study, then time eats away at the collective wisdom, both for individuals who neglect to apply themselves, and for the whole of humanity as well. This is how some of the sciences that formerly flourished among the ancients have been allowed to go downhill.

Commentary on the Ethics Book 1, lesson 11

6: The Virtuous Life

Reading through the articles of the *Summa Theologiae,* the Nobel laureate for poetry Sully-Prudhomme, who in his youth (it is said) thought of taking the same religious habit as St. Thomas, observed with discouragement: "That's so complicated! How did he get all of that out of the gospel, which is so simple?" This question is especially apt in the area of human destiny and behavior, where Thomas's inspired versatility and profound sense of mystery seem to dissolve into interminable rational investigations of the motives of moral action and the interrelationships of the virtues. The subtle, down to earth analyses of the Second Part of the *Summa* are a disappointment for a certain kind of mystical mentality.

Granted that there are legitimate differences of temperament, vocation, and literary genres; nonetheless, I need to criticize that "disappointment." It represents an attitude that is much too widespread. This "mystical" attitude imagines that the divine presence can only be manifested in irrationality—only where science (either human or physical) is impotent, where the unknowable is treated as the privileged locus of the divinity, and where social life is still under the power of the collective unconscious and religious instincts. In this view, when reason is in charge—personal reason or political judgment, the discernment of action or the practical techniques of human society—the influence of the gospel along with its sense of mystery just evaporates.

However, for Thomas Aquinas, by contrast, balance in the movement toward perfection is the surest moral sign of grace. Human wisdom represents the most perfect realization of the image of God, even given the powerful inspiration of the gospel. The virtuous life is the empire of reason.

"The Temptation of Christ" at Saulieu, early 12ᵗʰ cent.
From the Bourgogne Romane, *plate 75.*

VIRTUE IS REASON IN ACTION

Virtue is reason in action. An action performed by a person becomes properly human because of reason. *Only those actions which a person performs that are characteristic of his or her being human, are called human acts. Humans differ from nonreasoning creatures in this, namely, that they are the master of what they do . . . through their mind and their will. . . . Other actions that may be attributed to them can be called "acts of a person"* (actus hominis), *but not "human acts," since they are not precisely their own as human beings.*[1]

So human acts are virtuous to the degree that they are saturated with reason; this is so in all the aspects of behavior even down to its psychic underpinnings where our physiological reflexes engage passion. Christian experience teaches that humans never arrive at the point where they can take control of the very first movements of appetite. St. Thomas notes and analyzes these impulsive deviations not as faults expressly committed against a precept, but as the consequence of sense images that preclude the deliberation of reason.

St. Thomas was a demanding optimist. He thought that reason should be able to influence everything that arises spontaneously in our affections, not because of unyielding repression, but because of a mindfulness so habitual as to forestall surprises. This is the ideal state of humanity, and we find the prototype of it in the Bible's representation of Adam coming forth from the hands of the Creator in a euphoria linked to his experience of divine friendship.

But is that still a valid description of a human being? And isn't biblical realism closer to the mark when it describes the dramatic struggle of the human heart riven in two, unable to find balance and hope without the gracious deliverance of the Lord? Human beings as interpreted by St. Paul and St. Augustine, or by Pascal and Mauriac, are not impassive and angelic. Not at all!

The passions of the wise are not extinguished, but on the contrary maintain their full force. In the ideal order, both emotional and spiritual pleasures should attain their full intensity in ways radically different from the seductions of cheap excitement. True delight never experiences the bitter deception of sensual excess that fails to satisfy for long. True pleasure is not a useless and dubious accompaniment of indifferent acts, but rather the sign of good health and the normal

---

[1] *Summa Theologiae*, I–II, q. 1, art. 1.

effect of moral perfection, which is defined as happiness. In such happiness, the freedom of the sons and daughters of God is expressed.

This is neither dualistic Manichaeism nor Christian Stoicism. Pascal the Stoic certainly found his way to grace—but in the same century when both Erasmus and Luther, each in his own way, had disconnected grace from nature. Neither the generosity of Descartes or the good will of Kant leads to a balanced morality. It takes human reason enfleshed in ensouled matter, understood as God's gift to us, to become an instrument of the spirit leading to sound morality.

It happens often enough that reason is obliged to impose its perspective in conflict with rebellious appetites that insist upon their quest for pleasure, leading to an out-and-out combat. Nowadays the only part of this all too common situation that people pay attention to is defined by the word *duty,* which has come to represent the whole of morality. To act well means to conquer the self. The more the conquest is difficult or urgent, the more the act of the will is valued.

St. Thomas didn't deny either this experience or this kind of disharmony. But he refused to root human perfection in this embattled moral conflict. Rather he claimed that virtue can lead to a developed spiritual mastery in which the appetites delight in yielding to the enlightenment and the guiding imperatives of reason. Otherwise the human person would be lost in a moral insecurity that lacks ease and conviction in performing good actions. Such a condition of "continence" is not yet true virtue.

Is the human person divided? Of course. We recognize ourselves in this situation. But even in its difficult victories over passion, continence does not exhaust our nature or our goodness which are fulfilled only in an integrated humanity.

Reason's sovereign and subtle mastery is achieved not by becoming detached from surly appetites incapable of receiving the light of authentic goodness. No, rather the appetites themselves are supposed to become virtuous, and their sensibilities expand in the euphoria of their transformation. It is not by will power alone nor by superfluous intentions that spouses turn the actions of their state of life into virtue, that princes turn the magnanimity of their power into virtue, or that administrators of justice turn their revulsion and anger into virtue. In all these cases, virtue arises from the right ordering of their human acts. Adam, with his perfect moral equilibrium, experienced more conjugal pleasure than a sinner drunk with concupiscence; and

King St. Louis was more *imperial* holding court under the oak at his castle of Vincennes than the royal despot Frederick II.

In contrast to Bonaventure (and to many others after him down to our days), Thomas Aquinas held that the virtues of temperance and fortitude (as they are technically named) are seated not in the will but in the emotive powers of the sensitive appetites. The instincts, sensibilities, and tensions of the emotions are authentic elements of the virtuous life within the dynamic integrity of the human composite. These appetites come to participate in the dignity of reason, in the human (and for the Christian, divine) quality of our life. The moral writings of Corneille, Descartes, or Kant have lost this humanizing understanding of morality.

Let us take note of a technical precision in Thomas's psychological analysis of morality that will confirm the character of this equilibrium. In contrast to a spirit of supernaturalism, Thomas teaches that these moral virtues, at different levels of expression and having distinct roles to play, together create a unique human beauty. This is similar to the way culture provides a spiritual integrity for human life beyond the particular interests of different perspectives and fields of study. The dispositions of the intellect become linked to the virtues in the appetites in a human balance that in no way diminishes the role of grace or the supernatural virtues. This is not only because of the virtue of charity shaping them as if from the outside, but also because of the dynamic power of their own equilibrium.

This integrating power is rooted (even in the case of reason) in the primal and commanding will directed toward its ultimate end, shaping and rectifying the lower appetites toward its goal. For the Christian, the love of God will enlighten every discernment and will become the norm for every moral act, not withstanding the reasoning that internal or external circumstances will require. The rectitude of a human act, like the truth of the speculative intellect, is built upon the correct identification of its proper object. But here the moral reality can be identified and established only in and through a will fixed on its proper end and thus able to shape our free motions of choice and to surmount the inevitable fallibility of the human condition.

The rectitude of the appetites is not thereby deprived of objectivity, since the appetites still follow the directive force of nature. But the virtue of charity plays its indispensable role of resolving the kind of conflicts characteristic of the contingency with which reason must deal.

In contrast to Socratic intellectualism and the *Republic* of the Greek philosophers, Thomas teaches that practical truth is directed by the intentions, the convictions, and the judgments of human agents. But he opposed a morality of "good intentions" which (even under the cover of love) would leave out the structure of events, the rights of individuals, the objective laws of societies, and (in the conduct of princes) confer absolute power on the force of will. To do all that would be to scorn not only Socratic intellectualism but also the role of intelligence. Intellectual understanding, including the understanding of faith, is the rule of moral action as well as of human thought.

THE VIRTUE OF PRUDENCE

Should not the intellect itself be the seat of a virtue all its own in order to take control of human life? Shouldn't it supervise all the other virtues in some way, as well as the outward-turned emotions of love? Shouldn't it introduce into the sequence of our individual passing actions a governing light of rationality?

Here exactly is the decisive element of St. Thomas's account of moral life. It took him a long time to create it. And he was the only one among all his peers to do so. The originality of his ideas about prudence are still poorly understood and poorly integrated by both moral theologians and spiritual writers. The very name of this "intellectual" virtue in contemporary language indicates the loss of its doctrinal significance. Among moralists as well as in common usage, "prudence" is treated as of small account—as a simple habit of caution and calculation that provides a practical security and an uncertain know-how. The stature of prudence is hardly enhanced by its reputation for offering counsel with little to show in the way of human achievement.

But for Aristotle, the great theoretician of the life of wisdom, prudence has completely different qualities and a far richer significance. Prudence designates precisely the stable disposition thanks to which reason discerns, chooses, and commands, among the changing variety of our actions, their true ordination toward the ultimate end. This is practical truth which cannot be determined by general principles of science or wisdom, because it is truth immersed in the unique singularity of real actions and situations. It is experiential truth, then, but experience assured by the intentional movement of a being guided by a right relation of means to end—a relation that neither good intentions nor mystical passion can bring about.

Prudence does not constitute an additive to reason and will from outside in the way that a duty is imposed upon freedom to constrain its expression. Prudence is reason itself rendered perfect in its judgment and its choices. Prudence interiorizes and personalizes the law to the point that I am able to speak decisively about obligation only from inside my conscience. The virtuous are the living rule of their own action. Their reason owes the final determination of their action to the practical certitude of prudence.

This was Aristotle's idea, and St. Thomas followed him. But, we might ask, doesn't this picture of rational virtue put us outside the perspectives of the gospel . . . ? No, not so. There could be no more able, deferential, and objective translation of the pagan Aristotle's analysis than the one which Thomas makes as an evangelical theologian. Aristotelian prudence is focused upon experience—its particularities and its contingencies. In contrast to Platonism and its eternal ideas, Thomas accepts the inevitable concrete dimensions of human action. But he has prudence depend upon an inner light in the depths of the spirit, a spiritual light that constitutes the nature of prudence.

"Natural Law," providing instinctively the first principles of human agency, is a participation in the legislative wisdom of God rooted within the person. Here are found the highest inclinations of human nature—its tendency toward the Good, Truth, and Justice, and the inviolability of the human spirit. These moral inclinations are brought to bear upon contingent events without dissolving their transcendent value. These tendencies toward authentic Good constitute the goodness and stability of human nature. They express the presence of the Creator not only in my being, but in my acts.

Prudence is precisely the endowment through which my reason, true to itself, is able to govern the vast changeableness of my behavior and to refract into my most difficult actions the eternal divine attributes of Truth, Justice, and authentic fulfillment. The decisions of prudence are objective; they draw upon the light of all the virtues (as explained by moral science). The human agent is not the victim of circumstances. The deliberations of conscience in individuals and in history are the embodiment of divine governance extended toward contingent happenings in our ordinary world. Prudence comes to serve the interests of wisdom, our highest spiritual power, capable of knowing the ultimate Cause. The activity of prudence receives its definitive confirmation through its contemplation of this ultimate Cause. Prudential reason not only makes me human, but leads me to become more and more so, to the point of becoming reasonable—being an image of God.

Once God is revealed to me and invites me to communion in his life, then prudence, internally transformed by infused grace and enabled to guide me toward eternal life, receives its governing force from the divine object. Consequently the vision of faith and the conduct of moral acts converge into a practical synthesis.

Prudence directs the activity of the virtues toward eternal life. It places the unfolding of our work and our struggles under the light of a contemplation far distanced from the contingencies of human existence. Contemplatives are, within Thomas's understanding, persons of initiative, and nothing goes right in their lives that isn't linked in some way with contemplation. Plato's dream in the *Republic* finds its expression here in this communion of theory and practice and of the real and the rational—a condition that defines Christian wisdom.

However, this does not draw prudence away from its proper role. Having these transcendent connections and being empowered by its hope for eternal happiness, prudence still follows its appropriate norms and keeps to its task and its functional orientation. Its efficacy remains bound up with the ways and means of its practical knowledge. Neither divine nor human love dismantles its ways of acting or its resources. The gospel *moves through it*. Although the contemplative St. Thomas is a bit embarrassed by a certain religious extravagance or spiritual intoxication that is overwhelmed by the abundance of divine beatitude, he can nonetheless explicitly adopt (after a bit of Aristotelian interpretation) Augustine's definition: *Prudence is a love that chooses with sagacity.*[2]

CONSTRUCTING SOCIAL REALITY

Reason's mastery is expressed not only in its influence upon interior moral judgment and individual behaviors. The virtue of prudence extends to all the activities in which persons become engaged and where they meet others. It extends to the organization of society and even to the direction of the economy. Aristotle went so far as to consider political prudence as the perfect expression of the virtue. Political prudence is the virtue of the prince which considers the common good of the city-state and transcends the concerns of individuals.

[2] Ibid., II–II, q. 47, art. 1.

In this context, ambition seems to be paradoxical for the Christian, a problem presenting seemingly insurmountable obstacles. Doesn't the gospel itself renounce ambition and invest all its power in fraternal love, as if rational regulations were not even appropriate for bringing about order in our cities? Haven't Christians always been hesitant, indeed reserved, about structural reforms of society? Social justice aims to be (often in vain) both an objective law and a collective virtue.

Here once again, grace and nature embrace, in order to transcend the harmful separation so often at work in the popular imagination. The rational order of justice is not foreign to the gospel absolutes of charity, but is rather the extension of them. It would be a false charity that would refuse to become engaged in the needs of human communities and their social problems. The love that unites person to person in Christ and in society only becomes authentic if it achieves equality with the one loved. This equality confers on the loved one the rights that define and measure the objectivity of the virtue of justice. In the human community, politics is the supreme science. Further, political prudence is not only the quality of the leader, but also the virtue of the citizen whose obedience is only virtuous if it interiorizes a precept with a reasonable judgment in light of the common good.

Charity is political in its own way, beyond considerations of interpersonal reciprocity. The social and political demands of the public order are not dissolved under the influence of charity. It is by being Caesar that Caesar is a good servant of the gospel. *Ama et fac quod vis* ("Love and do what you will"): this admirable dictum of St. Augustine cannot disguise the limitations of an idealism which would skip over the demands and the structure of the human act. In contrast to Augustinian thinkers, St. Thomas held that if charity is the form of the virtues, this is not at the expense of their rational structure.

He understood that the virtues are moved to their proper object and are set in motion with the goal of reaching appropriate ends, especially in the area of the social virtues relating to justice. True love, even apostolic love, respects the order of things, the value of civic commitment, and the rhythms of history. Here Dominican theology distances itself from the spirituality based on "brotherhood" of the Friars Minor that eventually had repercussions on their institutions and apostolates because of its weak investment in moral rationality.

Thomas's confidence in reason extended down to the construction of the human environment that God entrusts to us. Placed as we are at the intersection of spirit and matter, our earthly destiny is to discover the reasonable laws of the cosmos through the theoretical and practical sciences and to order its energies using the technology that allows us bit by bit to govern the universe in view of the providential goals of a continuing creation.

This confrontation of the human with nature in which the history of civilizations is played out transcends questions of economic well-being. The higher question is how to achieve the conditions necessary for a totally human life. Economists have sometimes been dismayingly naive in their use of the rational methods of their pretentious discipline. A prophetic wit might have much to find amusing there. Aristotle would say that they confuse the means with the end. Their judgments lack prudence because of insufficient rational analysis. Still, their optimism is the expression of a correct (if too abrupt) conviction, namely, that nature is intelligible. Nature is full of ideas that I can draw forth from it, of causes that I can dominate. Progress is the happy result of this mastery.

Capital of pillar sculpted from limestone, a harpist (King David). From L'Esprit de Cluny, *plate 44.*

Progress in human endeavors as well as progress in social thought (whether about moral discernment or political structures) comes about through virtue and by way of rational analysis. Long before Hegel, Aristotle was able to emphasize the rationality of human and political values. The light of the gospel, through its reference to ultimate reality, keeps us from separating the rational order of nature and history from its ultimate significance. The separation of society from its divine destiny is the inverse of the view that takes interest in God only for the sake of manipulating the world.

So human progress takes its significance from what lies beyond it, even though this in no way diminishes its rational autonomy or its passionate involvement. In a kind of Promethean hubris, people can give in to the temptation of making an idol of human progress. But such a stupidity does violence to the Creator's plan. However, even this abuse of reason in its foolishness is still a testimony to human rationality, although we betray it when we deny its divine dimensions. Science is the daughter of God *(Deus scientiarum Dominus:* "God, the Lord of the Sciences")—the physical, psychological, and social sciences as well as the moral science of the individual. Sadly, this moral science (the work of prudence) can be too quickly accused of being naturalistic by proponents of philosophical or mystical voluntarism.

APOLLO OR DIONYSIUS?

Despite appearances, we are far away from the Greek idea of the human. The Greek sage—whether a disciple of Plato, Aristotle, Epictetus or Hermes Trismegistos—had no way of knowing how to ground contemplation in the unknowable divinity nor how to orient action toward the administration of secular government. More to the point, the sage had no way to balance the demands of action and contemplation. The Greek spirit was divided between the ecstasy of the Gnostic and the asceticism of the moralist, between the abandonment of reason in the dark pursuit of the eternal One and getting bogged down in attempts at political achievement. Greek wisdom was sometimes carried away by debauchery and at other times by magic. Sometimes the prisoner of its own logic and captive to its own demon in the pursuit of absolute clarity, the Greek spirit emphasized the divine quality of the Truth and the Good without being able to give them human expression. Even Socrates didn't escape from such ambiguity, despite the irony that he became its victim. Plato will degenerate into Neoplatonism, and Plotinus will overlook human history.

Nietzsche was intoxicated with the Greek myths. One after the other he exalted both Apollo—the eternal image of immovable and unique perfection—and Dionysius—whimsical and changeable in his habitual drunkenness; Nietzsche treated them like opposing forces as necessary to culture as the antagonism between the sexes is to humanity. Which one is fertile? Which one is creative? Neither, for neither Apollo nor Dionysius were creatures from God, much less sons of God, even though each in his way might have suggested thoughts of sacred marriage *(hieros gamos)* and divine union. But the human being is a creature, and God is the Creator freely pouring being forth into intelligences and freedoms that are being created in God's image and that construct that image in themselves. Here everything is turned around: the Greek world is turned upside down.

Even before our divine rebirth comes to expression through the mastery of grace, both practical reason and contemplative understanding already express God's idea for humanity and God's will for the world. God—far from being distant or jealous—accomplishes the eternal divine design in human beings and through them, so that we may lead the structures of our nature to their perfection and so that this universe may be constructed according to its true plan. God does this in a continuing creation that time neither wears down nor spoils.

Prudence is our participation in God's Providence, both eternal and temporal. It brings about not only the rational mastery of our human faculties, but also God's immanent delight in the unfolding of the smallest contingencies of our free human acts. God's mastery reaches down into the complexity of our physiological responses as well as into the economic and political aspects of our social life. The genius of the human creature comes from its balance: human asceticism is worked out in spiritual freedom so that a joyful face is the visible effect of nobility of soul and of divine grace.

Apollo or Dionysius? St. Thomas would not have seen either of these figures in the sculptures that were carved in stone over cathedral porticoes. If Thomas borrows something of their vague, seductive imagery from Aristotle or Hermes, it is not because of something drawn from their myths. If, besides Christ, there is one figure who represents Thomas's ideal of healthy, joyful equilibrium—someone balanced in himself, in the community of his friends, and in his understanding of political institutions—this is Brother Dominic, the founder of his order, the Master of the Preachers, and the witness to the gospel.

As Dominic's biographer, Jordan of Saxony, wrote:

"Dominic had a very strong nobility of soul. Because joy in the heart makes one's face full of joy, the serene equilibrium of his inner being was shown externally by expressions of his goodness and the happiness of his countenance. Dominic maintained a perfect consistency in the concerns that he judged reasonable to undertake, so that he never (or almost never) agreed to change a decision made after careful deliberation. In his ordinary routines, no one mixed in more than he in the social exchanges with his brothers and no one was more joyful. By his luminous expression, he won the love of everybody from the first glance. He always appeared as a man of the gospel, both by his words and his actions."[3]

THE PARADOX OF THE GOSPEL

Once again, in this delicate question of human agency, we observe that for St. Thomas the sign of the gospel's influence in history is the subtle harmony of grace and nature. Better, it is the perfecting of nature in and through grace. *Gratia non tollit naturam sed perficit* ("Grace does not diminish nature, but completes it").[4] This convergence can appear paradoxical to someone who has put faith in the great themes of the gospel, whether in the renunciation linked to the Cross of Christ or in the messianic perspective of an eschatology which discounts temporal affairs.

Everything that we have said before about speculative reason's constructing a theology in which reasoning nourishes faith and affords it an understanding of the Mystery believed—all that needs to be said over again here about practical reason. There is here a perfect homogeneity of doctrine and method. Prudence in the practical reason, by the light of its counsels and in the freedom of its choices, structures and personalizes the grace of my participation in divine life throughout the unfolding of my days and my circumstances.

It would be easy to collect references to give a biblical grounding to this virtue whose technical dynamics were identified by the pagan Aristotle. Here Aristotle is again put to the service of Christian anthropology in contrast to the Platonic idealism of philosophers and spiritual writers who, in their dismissal of the properties of human agency, hand over the direction of human behavior to some esoteric

---

[3] Jordan of Saxony, *Libellus on the Beginnings of the Order of Preachers*, op. cit., vol. 16, 74.

[4] *Summa Theologiae*, I, q. 1, art. 8, resp. 2.

mysticism. But authentically human behavior is constituted precisely by prudence, whose goal is to incarnate the mystery of God within both individual and social life. Prudence is a science of moral action.

The gospel absolutes lose nothing in being expressed in the available reality of human cooperation and freedom. On the contrary, a feverish pursuit of gospel purity would be an illusion if it failed to become immersed in the ephemeral concreteness of our moral acts. Both in human behavior and in human thought, grace gives nature the capacity to become fully itself, that is, a reasonable and free nature characterized by specific norms, values, structures, methods, and criteria.

Moral theology is and remains, like the whole of theology, a science about divine life. It forfeits nothing of its high dignity when its proper object becomes this divine life expressed within my human acts. Moreover, moral theology in no way gives way to a dualism of theory and praxis (to which philosophy so often succumbs). It remains unified and unifying under the light of faith which, in daily communion with the life of God, is the living truth of the gospel. This light has the power to illumine both my thoughts as well as my actions.

Church of the Sorbonne, Firma Lévy et Neurdein, Paris.

TEXTS

Virtue is the Work of Reason

A virtue is a perfection added to a power of the soul. The perfection of anything, however, is considered principally with respect to its relationship to its end or goal. The end or goal of a power is its exercise in action. So we call a power perfect when it is well determined toward its act.

Some powers are determined toward their proper act on their own, such as naturally active powers [as contrasted with voluntary ones]; and such powers deserve the name virtue. However, the rational powers that are distinctive of the human are not determined to one single kind of operation, but remain open to multiple forms of operation. They are oriented to their acts through habits, and that is why we call human virtues "habits."

Summa Theologiae I–II, q. 55, art. 1

. . . There is a sort of disposition toward virtue that results from the natural inclination of the individual and through which some persons find themselves disposed to exercise a certain virtue by reason of their natural constitution. This kind of inclination is certainly a sort of beginning of virtue, but we have to say that it is not really perfect virtue, since perfect virtue implies that the rule of human reason already has been established in the personality. This is why we include in the definition of virtue that it chooses means to action *according to right reason.* For if people were to follow this kind of inclination [from their natural constitution] without reasonable discernment, they would often sin. So considered, this beginning of virtue without the guidance of reason does not constitute authentic virtue.

We must say the same [about other natural aptitudes, spiritual powers, or passions]. Look at the intellect: when we draw particular conclusions from universal principles, this is because of the action of reason. Look at the will: it is once again thanks to the help of reason that we find ourselves led from desire to our ultimate end by means that are appropriate to this end. Finally, with respect to the passions: it is reason itself that controls the emergency and pleasure-seeking emotions [the irascible and concupiscible] and brings them under reason's mastery.

It is clear therefore that the help of reason is needed for virtue to be established, whether it is the case of virtue in the intellect, in the will, in the emergency passions or in the pleasure-seeking passions. And here is what virtue's establishment consists in: the disposition toward virtue that exists in a superior faculty becomes applied to develop virtue in an inferior part of the person. This happens, for example, when we are made ready for a virtue in the will by both the disposition in the will itself as well as by the disposition toward virtue that exists in the intellect. Similarly, we are made ready for virtue in the irascible and concupiscible passions both by the beginnings of virtue that can be found in these powers as well as by the beginning of virtue that exist in the higher powers of the personality. However, the higher powers are never led to virtue by the beginnings of virtue in the lower powers. In this way, reason, which is the highest of human powers, helps all the other powers to reach the full amplitude of virtue in their own domains. . . . So the perfection of virtue does not come from nature, but from reason.

Disputed Question on the Virtues, q. 1, art. 8

The Rectification of the Passions

If we were to agree with the Stoics that the human passions are disordered affectivity, then we would have to say that perfect virtue excludes the passions. However, if we take the passions to mean all the movements of the sensitive appetites, then it is clear that the moral virtues that govern the passions as their proper object cannot exist without these passions. The reason for this is that otherwise moral virtue would create the result of rendering the sensitive appetite totally idle or useless. But virtue's function is not to deprive the powers that virtue subjects to reason of their proper acts, but rather to have them execute the command of reason when they express the acts proper to them. Therefore, just as virtue directs the physical parts of the body to their proper external acts, so also it directs the sensitive appetite to the acts proper to it.

However, the moral virtues that are not concerned with governing the passions but with social actions [*operationes*] can exist without these passions. The virtue of justice is like that, because through justice the will is applied to its specific act, which does not involve the passions. Note, however, that joy follows upon performing an act of justice, at least in the will (and in that case it is not passion). But if this joy is multiplied by reason of the perfecting of the act of justice, it will overflow into the sensitive appetite by reason of the fact that the lower powers follow the lead of the higher powers of the personality.

As a result of this sort of overflowing of joy, the more perfect a virtue is, the more it will engender a response within the passions.

Summa Theologiae, I–II, q. 59, art. 5

Prudence and Wisdom

Since prudence concerns human affairs and wisdom by contrast is concerned with the highest Cause, it is not possible for prudence to be a greater virtue than wisdom; unless, as Aristotle states in his *Ethics* (VI, 7, 1141a21), *the human beings were considered the greatest of everything that exists in the universe.* So the same book says that prudence does not govern wisdom, but rather vice versa. Likewise Paul says in 1 Corinthians 2:15, "the spiritual person judges everything and is judged by no one." So prudence does not get involved in the highest things which are the concern of wisdom, but rather governs matters that are subordinated to wisdom, namely, how people ought to go about attaining wisdom. In this way, prudence or political virtue is the servant of wisdom, because prudence prepares the path for wisdom, a bit like the doorkeeper prepares the way for the king.

Furthermore, we should note that prudence attends to the means for achieving happiness, while wisdom attends to the very object of happiness (the supreme truth). If the consideration of wisdom with respect to its object were perfect, then there would be perfect happiness in the act of wisdom. However, since the act of wisdom in this earthly life is imperfect with respect to its principal object, namely God, therefore the act of wisdom is just a beginning of or participation in future happiness. Still wisdom is closer to happiness than prudence is.

Summa Theologiae I–II, q. 66, art. 5, resp. 1 and 2

Freedom, Law, and Discipline

As noted elsewhere, while the human person has a natural aptitude toward virtue, the perfecting of virtue necessarily requires some kind of education for its complete acquisition. We can see that persons take care of the necessities that they need for life, such as food and clothing, by their industry. Nature provides humans their reasoning and manual dexterity, but not the products that they need; whereas nature provides the other animals sufficient nourishment and covering. With respect to educating people in virtue, it is not easy to find those who are self-sufficient, since developed virtue consists principally in restraining a person from inappropriate pleasures, to which people are especially prone, particularly the young for whom moral education is more effective. Therefore it is essential that people receive from others the education that leads them to virtue.

Now for young people who are inclined to acts of virtue because of good dispositions owing to nature or to habit or even to divine favor, a fatherly discipline of good advice will suffice. But other young people are either impudent, prone to vice, or not easily moved by admonitions; these have to be inhibited from evil acts by force or by fear so that at least they will stop doing evil and let others live in peace. They finally may find themselves led by the force of habit to do willingly what they earlier did only out of fear, and in this way they can become virtuous. The discipline of human law is like this kind of education which constrains people by the fear of punishment.

So we can see that laws are needed to assure social peace and to foster virtue. This is why Aristotle says that, "Just as human persons, if perfect in virtue, are the best of all the animals; so also when they are separated from law and justice, they become the worst" (*Politics*, I, 1: 1253a31). For humans can use the weapons of reasoning, which other animals don't have, to fight against lust and brutality.

Summa Theologiae I–II, q. 95, art. 1

The Virtue of Prudence

Prudence is made up of several components:

- the memory of past experiences,
- an inner feeling for a particular end or goal,
- docility toward the wise and toward more experienced persons,
- careful attention to circumstances,
- determined exploration using reasoning that perseveres,
- the consideration of future possibilities,
- the assessment of opportunities, and
- taking care to avoid obstacles.

Following that, these, too, are components of prudence:

- good counsel from a reason that is well ordered,
- right judgment about particular actions, and
- the ability to discern conditions in which exceptions must be made.

Summa Theologiae II–II, qq. 48, 49, 51 passim.

7: The Fate of St. Thomas

In reading the impassive moral analysis of the *Summa Theologiae*, you might never guess the fevered atmosphere in which these university lectures and their corresponding texts were developed. However, some echoes of the conflict remain in the edited versions of these debates (*quaestiones disputatae* "disputed questions"). St. Thomas's allusions not only let us identify historical texts and personalities with whom he was engaged in dispute, but also make us aware of the deep divisions of opinion about the relationship of reason and faith and of nature and grace that underlie the conflict of the reported positions.

A curious coalition developed as Aristotelian rationalism penetrated more and more deeply into the Faculty of Arts and as Thomas Aquinas's new theological method became more successful. The former chancellor of the University of Paris, Stephen Tempier, became the bishop of Paris in 1268. He was unswervingly attached to conservativism in the schools. He joined up with Bonaventure, whose Augustinian bent (apparently more congenial to the spirit of St. Francis) never agreed with the rational autonomy of the method of his colleague Thomas Aquinas. Thomas, as a common enemy, brought them together.

In addition, the "philosophers" claimed for themselves a definitive purely secular wisdom for which faith and its mysteries were neither important nor helpful. Brought up on Averroes, Siger of Brabant, Boethius of Dacia, and others like them (without holding the theory of two truths which Tempier accused them of holding) tended to separate faith in the gospel from secular behavior (including the moral virtues, politics, and the place of humanity in the world). In this approach we see reflected the cosmic humanism and the rational search for happiness that is characteristic of Greek philosophy.

Bell tower from the monastery church of Cluny in France,
12ᵗʰ cent. From L'Esprit de Cluny *plate 1.*

The Cistercian Abbey of Le Thoronet, 12ʰ cent., from the Bourgogne Romane, *plate 80.*

Their use of Aristotelian epistemology, which created a hierarchy of autonomous disciplines treating spirit and action, led them to this unhealthy dualism. One of the most harmful effects of their position was that it denied faith its right and its capacity to become integrated with reason into a wisdom enlightened by divine light. They didn't think that theology was capable of achieving this integration or of enjoying this rational freedom midway between pure gospel inspiration and simple obedience to revealed teaching.[1]

We can see how Thomas Aquinas found himself compromised in the investigation of errors that condemned "equivocal expressions dangerous for those of simple faith" (as the accusation put it). A syl-

[1] Étienne Gilson, "Boèce de Dacie et la double vérité," *Archives d'histoire doctrinale et littéraire du moyen âge* 22 (1955) 81–99.

labus of 219 propositions in reaction to the growing rationalism and naturalism of the time was both a legitimate act of authority and simplistic in its perspective: in 1277 it condemned twenty propositions among which were included methodological principles of the Dominican Master.

Thomas had been dead for three years before this long episode culminated in the condemnation. He had died on his way to the ecumenical Council of Lyons (1274), having been summoned by the Holy See to be a trusted advisor to the council fathers. The condemnation of 1277 provoked a bitter reaction among his disciples, at the Faculty of Arts in Paris as well as among theologians and his Dominican confreres. The Masters of Arts had publicly displayed their devotion and attachment to Thomas by requesting of the Friars Preachers that his mortal remains be buried at the University of Paris, which they considered the only place worthy to receive him. Likewise, they asked for his last writings to be given to them.

Qualified theologians, even those who had never been disciples of the Dominican Master, denounced the summary procedures of the condemnation and the confusions characteristic of this kind of document. Though legitimate, the pastoral reaction against the genuine dangers for Christian thought and behavior flowing from the widespread naturalism of many thinkers had not been able to carefully sort through all the partisan theological positions.

In any case, the prohibition against taking the positions of Brother Thomas was promptly reversed, to the astonishment of many, despite the "corrections" developed by the Franciscan school. Aquinas's reputation remained intact with the Holy See as both a religious and a theologian of integrity, and this reputation was to be affirmed more and more publicly. His canonization, proclaimed by Pope John XXII in 1323, specified the motivation of his excellence in sacred teaching. This would forever ratify the authority of Thomas as a "doctor" of the Church.

Artists would come to celebrate the "triumph" of St. Thomas, using the resources of the traditions of iconography with their typical oversimplifications to illustrate solemn texts of the Church. We can feel free to enjoy these images, provided that they do not make us forget the serene discipline, the technical methodology, and the inspired freedom of the spiritual choices that made Thomas Aquinas a Master Preacher.

The posthumous history of the theology of St. Thomas, at once both glorious and controversial, is of interest not just for those attracted

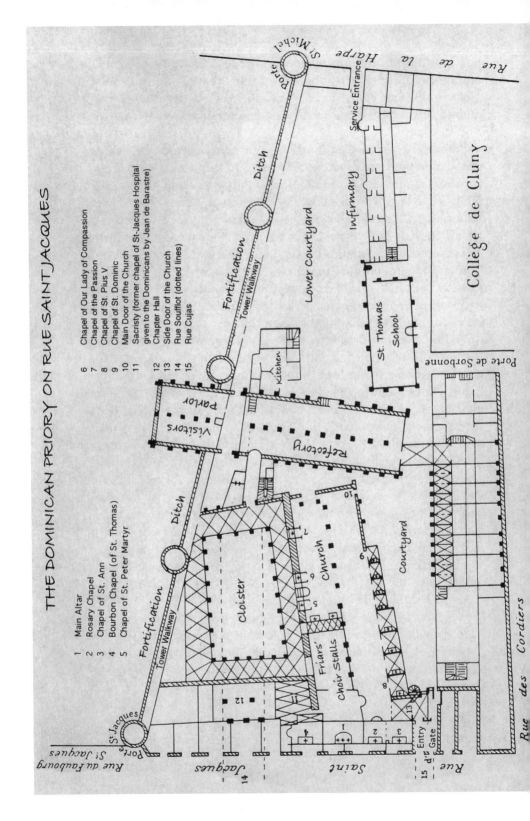

THE DOMINICAN PRIORY ON RUE SAINT JACQUES

1 Main Altar
2 Rosary Chapel
3 Chapel of St. Ann
4 Bourbon Chapel (of St. Thomas)
5 Chapel of St. Peter Martyr
6 Chapel of Our Lady of Compassion
7 Chapel of the Passion
8 Chapel of St. Pius V
9 Chapel of St. Dominic
10 Main Door of the Church
11 Sacristy (former chapel of St-Jacques Hospital
   given to the Dominicans by Jean de Barastre)
12 Chapter Hall
13 Side Door of the Church
14 Rue Soufflot (dotted lines)
15 Rue Cujas

to pious or academic triumphalism. As with other great thinkers, the heritage of Aquinas developed into certain masterpieces of doctrinal expression through the progressive clarifications that came out of new historical contexts and fresh theoretical polemics. We are left with a tradition that our own age must assess in order to discover its significance and draw out its theoretical and pastoral usefulness.

Without going into the details of this long and complex history, let me remark that the first half of the twentieth century contributed a renewed appreciation for the full contribution of the theology of St. Thomas as a spiritual master. Off and on, there were occasions in which the value and conclusions of his philosophy were highlighted. Disputes among schools of both spirituality and scholastic thought had led some thinkers to consider St. Thomas as a "speculative" doctor, whose thought needed to be complemented by a "mystical" theology drawn from other sources, following different spiritual charisms. And we should note that the Church has always allowed freedom of expression for various schools of spirituality and has even canonized their representative leaders. Clearly, the mystery of God cannot be expressed in the thought forms of any single thinker.

Nonetheless, the truth of Catholic doctrine as well as a true reading of history insist that we do not break spiritual teaching away from its theological substructure. Theology is one reality, otherwise it risks being ripped away from the frame of the gospel upon which it is woven. As a son of Dominic, the *vir evangelicus* ("man of the gospel"), Thomas Aquinas is a spiritual master even in laboring scientifically at his theological work.

The Dominican Priory on Rue Saint Jacques. Inside back jacket cover, M.-D. Chenu, St Thomas d'Aquin et la théologie.

TEXTS

Against the Condemnation of Thomas Aquinas

There are people who delight in condemning as errors the opinions of their theological colleagues who articulate the faith and enlighten the Church. Precipitous action, however, means peril for the faith. The work of theologians, thanks to which we advance on the pathway of truth, calls for well-intentioned and free corrective responses, not exasperating detractions. Further, we should not impose a uniformity of opinion on all our disciples, because our intelligence is not supposed to be docile to the teaching of any human teacher, but only to the teaching of Christ. To claim, then, that the propositions of these theologians are errors, is to put the faith in peril by linking it to the weakness of our human understanding.

. . . Let the censors be still. If they choose to hold a contrary opinion, so be it. But they shouldn't judge other opinions to be erroneous. To do so is both precipitous judgment and spiritual weakness since, in their pride, they show both that they were unable to understand the decisive arguments at issue and that their own reasons were feeble.

Giles of Rome, "On the Physics of Aristotle and the Treatise on the
Unity of Forms" (Venice, 1502, fol. 206)

N.B.: Giles was forced not only to make a public apology but also to endorse the condemnation of Brother Thomas in order to be installed as Master in Theology at the University of Paris in 1285.

The Reputation of Saint Thomas as a Spiritual Master

Both in his teaching and in his writings about divine realities, Thomas Aquinas gives theologians an outstanding witness to the absolutely necessary link that exists between study and the spiritual senses of the soul. Someone who knows a distant place only by its description (however minutely described), does not really know it in truth. Only someone who has lived there truly knows it. In a similar way, scientific investigation cannot produce an intrinsic knowledge of God unless it arises from a close and vital union with God.

Pope Pius XI, Encyclical *Studiorum ducem* (1923)

Attentive to the infinite loftiness and freedom of the Creator, on the one hand, and to the radical contingency of created being, on the other, the doctrine of St. Thomas—thanks to a healthy understanding of universals, of the value of nature and the natural law (showing that under the gaze of God this nature remains completely responsive and perfectible as well as completely open to divine initiatives)—reduces to absurdity the naturalistic postulate and the hypocritical metaphysics (hidden under the surface of the positivistic sciences) that try to confer on the creature a divine autonomy *(aseity)*.

Understanding everything which the notion of "rational animal" signifies with respect to both greatness and limitation, situating human intelligence at the lowest degree on the scale of spiritual beings, rejecting all its claims to act as a pure spirit, Aquinas destroys at the root (at its angelic-seeming root) an individualism that effectively sacrifices the human person to an image of the human that is really illusory and destructive.

St. Thomas directs human intelligence to its proper object, orientates it to its proper end, and returns it to its true nature: this is the immediate benefit of his teaching. He tells human intelligence that it is made for *being*. . . . Submissive to its true object in order to achieve its authentic freedom in a spontaneous and lively way, human intelligence appropriates its essential hierarchies and the right order of its virtues.

Jacques Maritain, "Conference at Avignon in 1923 on the occasion of the sixth centenary of the canonization of St. Thomas"

It would be fruitless to look for an underlying "interior life" within Thomism whose essence would be specifically different from Thomism itself. It would be wrong to suppose that the learned structure of the *Summa Theologiae* and the progressive work of reason that built this immense edifice stone by stone were the products of superficial work on St. Thomas's part beneath which lay a richer, deeper, and more religious vision. St. Thomas's interior life—to the degree that the secret of such a powerful personality can be revealed to us—seems to have been exactly what it would have to be in order to be expressed as it is in his teaching.

Nothing more complicated nor nothing more passionate is needed beyond these demonstrations crafted from precisely defined ideas, organized into perfectly lucid formulations, and balanced into a rigorously ordered theological development. This kind of mastery in the expression and organization of philosophical ideas cannot be obtained without a total gift of oneself. The *Summa Theologiae* with its abstracted limpidity and its impersonal transparency is the expression of the interior life of St. Thomas Aquinas, crystallized under our eyes and stabilized forever.

If you want to evoke what is most profound and intense in this work, you can do nothing better than grasp the order that Thomas imposed upon the many diverse elements of his enormous project, study their internal relationships, and engender in yourself an understanding of how each fits properly into its required place. Only this kind of deep desire to understand, awakened in us by the author's own passion for order, will permit us to experience that his intellectual light is the blossoming of a well-ordered spiritual passion. Only this desire will allow us to rediscover beneath the orderly ideas the powerful effort that assembled them together into his teaching.

Only in this way can Thomism be appreciated in all its beauty. This philosophy moves us through its pure ideas, yielding to faith in the evaluation of its proofs and to selflessness before the rigors of reasoning. This aspect of his teaching will be more understandable to those beginners for whom Thomas's work constitutes heavy and difficult reading, if they remember that this was his religious spirituality. If it had been true that Thomas's teaching was informed by a different spirit than was his religious life, then we ought to be able to grasp the difference by comparing the way he prayed with the way he thought.

But look at the prayers of Thomas that have been preserved for us (whose religious spirit is so profound that the Church has inserted them into the Breviary), and you will easily note that their fervor is not marked by affective exaltation, passionate exclamations, or a taste for spiritual delights such as characterize other ways of praying. Rather, the fervor of St. Thomas is expressed completely through his desire to ask from God everything that he ought to ask for in the manner that is fitting. Here is genuine fervor that is deep and sensitive despite its rigorous expression in rhythmic balance and linguistically graceful formulas. But it is the fervor of a spirituality in which everything moves according to the right order and the rhythm of reasonable thinking.

"I pray that this holy communion may not be a cause for punishment, but a saving intercession for my pardon. Let it be for me a shield of faith and a sword of good will. May it destroy my vices, exterminate my concupiscence and lust, and cause my growth in love and patience, humility and obedience, and all the virtues. Let it be a strong protection against the bad influence of my enemies (both visible and invisible). May it bring about the perfect quieting of my carnal and spiritual urges. Finally may this communion give me firm commitment to You, my one and true God, and be the consummation of my life's final meaning."

This kind of spirituality is less interested in feeling than it is desirous of light. The rhythm of the phrases and the sonority of the words in no way changes the clear order of ideas. Nonetheless, can't anyone with sensitivity perceive beneath the staid expressions of Thomas's prayers not only religious emotion, but also a sort of poetry?

Étienne Gilson, *Thomisme* (fourth edition, Paris, 1942) 499.

8: The Works of St. Thomas

The writings of St. Thomas are, with a few exceptions, entirely productions required by his university teaching. Their literary form and technical style can only be understood as expressions of the interests, methodology, and pedagogy of that time.

The *quaestio disputata* ("disputed question") is Thomas's form for teaching and writing. This was the university's style of expression *par excellence* in its programs of higher studies. Beginning with the reading of source texts in all areas of study, from the *pagina sacra* of the Bible to treatises on medicine, "questions" were raised about both facts and doctrines. Based upon that, a *disputatio* or debate ensued between qualified Masters both "for" and "against" the point under discussion. Finally one of them "determined" the question so examined, that is, presented his conclusions in a clear and organic fashion.

The *quaestio* was the fruit of a long development in the twelfth century. By the middle of the thirteenth century, the disputed question had prevailed over the simple *lectio* (commentary) on the texts and had become the quintessential act of a Master, to the great disappointment of textual conservatives. We can easily imagine, even from this distance, the intellectual vitality and passionate involvement that such a communitarian pedagogy brought about, even within the study of theology.

In the view of his contemporaries, Thomas Aquinas excelled at this type of *disputatio* both because of his masterful serenity and because of his vigorous lucidity. His greatest work is not the *Summa Theologiae,* but rather his long series of *Quaestiones disputatae.* They should be read not only as a methodological curiosity or for their orderly pedagogy, remarkable as those aspects of his work are. Rather we should see them as the very definition of theological mastery—the Word of God is here submitted to rational investigation in a way that makes its questioning a profound homage to faith and its awareness of

Manuscript of Thomas Aquinas's De veritate, *13ᵗʰ cent.*

its divine object. This faithful questioning is the most acute expression of the life of the spirit.

Someone once protested that this sort of rational investigation of the faith was inappropriate and that it ought to give way to pure and simple obedience to God's authority. To this, Aquinas responded trenchantly: Of course, by giving in to authority, you will have the truth; but you will have the truth that way with an empty head!

This riposte is borrowed from a *disputatio* of a different kind, one called *de quodlibet* (freely chosen topics). Twice in the course of the university's academic year, just before Christmas and Easter, there was a solemn convocation at which the *disputatio* was not on a prepared and previously announced topic given by one of the professors, but rather on a topic chosen by the gathered university crowd who, according to their whim and will, put on the table the most diverse assortment of problems, ranging from questions of high metaphysical interest to matters of recent local experience. The Master was obliged to respond to each question and then, the next day, to "determine" (i.e., solve) the questions by organizing them according to the outcome of the discussions. St. Thomas has left us twelve disputations of this *de quodlibet* variety—all of them held in Paris. (Numbers VII to XI come from the years 1256–59. Numbers I–VI and XII come from the years 1269–72.)

Aquinas's "Disputed Questions" are classified and entitled according to the major theme of each one of the series. So we have *De veritate* ("On Truth"), twenty-four disputations at Paris between 1256 and 1259; then *De potentia* ("About Potency"), ten disputations from Italy between 1259 and 1268. The *Quaestiones disputatae De malo* ("On Evil") contain sixteen disputations conducted in Paris between 1269 and 1272, as were also the *De anima* ("On the Soul"), *De virtutibus* ("On the Virtues"), *De unione Verbi incarnati* ("On the Union of the Incarnate Word"), *De spiritualibus creaturis* ("About Spiritual Creatures"), and some other isolated disputed questions.

The "article," the basic unit for writing up these texts, makes evident the lively dialogue that underlay the text. The text needs to be read with an appreciation for this highly original context in order to understand the genre, the structure, and the conclusions of the article. In each article, there is a series of objections "for" and "against" that set up the disputed position of the problem being examined, then the citation of an "authority" who is more or less decisive of the question, followed by the determination (which forms the corpus or central portion of the article), and finally the responses to the arguments posed at the beginning.

The *Summa Theologiae* is not the outcome of teaching, but a work motivated by personal considerations (see below). Although the *Summa* was built upon the format of articles, in this case the form has been simplified considerably.

In addition, the older *lectio* (commentary or exposition) of source texts also prompted a good number of publications from St. Thomas. First, in Scripture, since the classic course of the Masters in Theology was and remained the literary and doctrinal exegesis of the *pagina sacra* of the Bible. Only his commentaries on Isaiah, Jeremiah, the Psalms, the book of Job, and the Song of Songs (?) in the Old Testament, and on the Gospels of Matthew and John and on the epistles of Paul, in the New Testament, have been preserved from this form of Aquinas's teaching.

These commentaries represent a type of theological exegesis that followed scholastic and symbolic norms largely foreign to our modern religious mentality. In addition to preserving this form of exegesis, these commentaries also constitute a biblical theology. Thomas Aquinas interprets the texts and their facts in the light of his coherent understanding of the divine economy (God's plan for the world), articulating the unfolding of God's intentions and initiatives, and their gradual expression through time. This is truly *doctrina sacra* (holy teaching).

The development of theological education had little by little introduced the *Liber Sententiarum* (Book of Sentences) of Peter Lombard (+1160) as a text for beginning professors, in order to initiate them into the teaching of Scripture. St. Thomas as a young professor had commented on it. However his commentary goes well beyond a mere analytical reading of the text and turns into the form of "questions." This is why this early work is so significant, since we find there his first expression of key principles for his thought.

His commentary upon the classical text of Boethius' *De Trinitate* ("On the Trinity") is constructed in the same fashion. This appears to be a manifesto about his methodology for a variety of spiritual disciplines, including sacred Scripture. Apparently Thomas's initiative in commenting on this text remained an isolated phenomenon not followed by others.

Denis (the Areopagite) was a famous Greek doctor who was an object of great curiosity because of translations recently done in

Thomas's time. Was his commentary on Denis a customary exercise for university professors? We don't know. But in any case, he followed the example of his Master Albertus Magnus in commenting on a text that was a totally different kind of "authority" for theology than the writings of Aristotle. The Dionysian corpus of writings were saturated with sayings of St. Maximus (the Greek Father) and grounded in his kind of theology. We find the text of Aquinas's course on the *De divinis nominibus* ("The Divine Names") inside an exposition on the literal text of this writing of Denis.

St. Thomas also explains the texts of Aristotle using a literal commentary, without going off into the form of questions. Albertus Magnus, to the scandal of more than a few, had introduced the *lectio* of the works of Aristotle (although forbidden) into public teaching. We have the compilation of Albert's teaching on Aristotle of which one part (the Ethics) is written in the hand of Thomas Aquinas, his pupil. Thomas followed the example of his Master at a time when the circulation of the works of Averroes, the most important of Aristotle's commentators, required a closer attention to the interpretation of the text and not just a simple paraphrase. Thomas's reading of Aristotle still has value for its exegetical and theoretical precision, even after the contributions of modern philologists. We have commentaries by Thomas on major works of Aristotle treating logic, physics, psychology, metaphysics, ethics, and politics (unfinished). These date for the most part from the second part of Thomas's career during the fiercest days of the Averroist crisis.

There are some forty works owed to special circumstances (traditionally called *opuscula* "little works"); some of these are quite important. An example is the short treatise *De esse et essentia* ("On Existence and Essence"), dedicated in 1265 to his younger colleagues among the professors. His *Compendium theologiae* ("Compendium of Theology") he dedicated to his secretary and friend, Reginald of Piperno. The *Summa contra Gentiles,* of which we have already seen the origin and significance above, holds a place of eminence among works that are not in the forms of disputed questions.

Finally, as we had occasion to observe, the Master in Theology also had to preach. Naturally he preached to the university community. And we have several series of Thomas's sermons (called *collationes*). They are in the form of summary notes and don't have the same significance as the sermons of his colleague Bonaventure, who was Master and Regent of the university college of Friars Minor.

St. Thomas became aware that the two forms of university teaching, the commentary on texts and the disputed questions, could not satisfactorily meet one of the essential requirements of theological education, namely, an organic presentation of the whole of sacred wisdom. This is how towards the end of his life he came to imagine writing a *summa* (summary) outside of the routine of his teaching. This means not a "manual," but a concise exposition of the teaching of theology adapted to the level of the general culture of the students and constructed on a plan that made clear the internal relationships of the objects under consideration. It is this last element, so significant in the *Summa Theologiae,* that warrants the somewhat romantic comparison between *summas* and cathedrals—both significant products of medieval civilization.

In both cases it is clear that the plan on which each is built is of the greatest significance. By examining the inner movement of the work that goes beyond its logical divisions and subdivisions, we can discover something of the intuitions of the master and his deepest intellectual proclivities. The impossibility of enclosing the object of theology—God's inner mystery and the divine economy of creation and salvation—within any plan, makes the options adopted all the more decisive. Within theology, scientific wisdom collides not only with the mystery of faith, but also with the radical contingency of facts within a history of salvation.

To overcome these obstacles, Thomas adopted the great Platonic theme of emanation and return. Since theology is the "science" (certain knowledge) of God, we have to study all things in their relation to God, whether with respect to their original production or to their final destiny. The theme of emanation and return provides intelligibility to the project both at the human level (where humans are understood to be cooperators with and images of the divine Architect) and in terms of a vision of the universe and a conception of nature. But it also proves to be open to history, in contrast to the determinism of the Greeks, by situating the facts and events of sacred history within the trajectory of emanation and return.

This is the nature of the *Summa's* construction and the shape of the movement that it describes. The *Prima Pars* (First Part) treats the emanation of reality from God as from its principle; the *Secunda Pars* (Second Part) treats reality's return to God as its destiny and goal. And because in fact according to God's free and gratuitous choice (as salvation history reveals to us) this return is achieved through Christ the man-God, a *Tertia Pars* (Third Part) examines the "Christian" conditions of this return. Historical reality will be in charge here even more than elsewhere, since history will be *revealing* in the strict sense of the word. Theological speculation will find its integrity by following the contingent mercies of divine love.

We can see here how theology remains religious knowledge even within its rational organizational schemes. Each of its elements is intrinsically referred to God and to the Word of God by reason of its situation within the theological program. It is not philosophical categories that assure unity to the program as if from outside, turning it into a kind of sacred metaphysics seasoned with spiritual allusions and pious corollaries. The divine mystery is intrinsic to this theology.

It would be a deadly misunderstanding (particularly in the Second Part of the *Summa*) to concentrate exclusively on the details of the Aristotelian structure of the work in a rigid and systematic way, while forgetting or skipping over the life-giving sap that comes from the Gospels and the Fathers. The Aristotelian framework is not accidental to the theology of the *Summa*, of course; no more than Platonic ideas are accidental to the theology of Augustine, Denis, and Gregory of Nyssa.

However, the systematic spirit of Thomas's work is made to respect at all cost the strange logic of the kingdom of God, whose designs are expressed as much in the secrets of divine mystery (and in the reverses of history) as in the happy outcomes of our hopes (and the success of the established Church). Theology always remains *doctrina sacra* (sacred teaching): it always seeks its answers in the gospel. Ultimately theology finds its fulfillment in the Word of God.

CULTURE AT THE TIME OF ST. THOMAS

1200		Charter of the University of Paris granted by Philip Augustus
1205–15	Foundation of the Friars Preachers	
1209	First Community of Franciscan Friars	
1210		Prohibition of Teaching Aristotle in the Schools
1214		Battle of Bouvines: setback for the Holy Roman Empire
1215	The Lateran Council	First Statutes of the University of Paris. In England, the Magna Carta
		Foundation of the Order of Mercedarians for the redemption of captives
1224 (25)	Birth of Thomas Aquinas	
1225		The "Canticle of the Sun" of St. Francis Assisi
1229		Foundation of the University of Toulouse (with public teaching of Aristotle): Dominican professors
1231		Louis IX grants corporate autonomy to the University of Paris (an act endorsed by the pope). Reminder that Aristotle is forbidden at the University
1234		The "Decretals" of Dominican Raymond of Peñafort

1239–44	Thomas Aquinas studies at the University of Naples	
1240		Beginning of the infiltration of the works of Averroes
1240–48		Albertus Magnus teaches at Paris, commenting on Aristotle. Roger Bacon comments on works of Aristotle
1243–45		Construction of *La Sainte Chapelle* in Paris
1244–45	Thomas enters the Order of Preachers: kidnapped, detained, then released	
1245–48	Thomas studies at Paris	
1246		The Franciscan John of Plano Carpini goes to the court of Mongolia
1248		Albertus Magnus founds the Faculty of Theology in Cologne
1248–52	Thomas studies at Cologne	
1248–54		The Crusade of King St. Louis
1248–55		Bonaventure teaches in Paris
1250		Dominicans establish schools for the study of Arabic
1259–70		Progressive influence of Averroes in the universities
1252		The gold Florin issued in Florence
1252–57		The theologians of Paris in conflict with the mendicants

1254		*Speculum naturale historiale* of Vincent of Beauvais, O.P.
1254–56	Thomas writes *Commentary on the Sentences*	
1254–80	Rutebeuf	
1256	Thomas, Master of Theology	
1257		Robert de Sorbon founds a college at the University of Paris
1258–60	Thomas writes the *Summa contra Gentiles*	
1259–68	Thomas teaches in Italy	
1260		Portico of the Virgin finished at Notre-Dame cathedral in Paris
1262–80		The musical plays of Adam de la Halle
1263		Reminder of the condemnation of Aristotle. William of Moerbecke translates Aristotle for St. Thomas
1266–68		Roger Bacon writes his three *Opera*
1266–70		The Averroist crisis: Siger de Brabant
1267–73	Thomas writes the *Summa Theologiae*	
1268–72	Thomas teaches in Paris	
1270		First condemnation of Averroism
1272–74	Thomas teaches at Naples	

1274	Thomas dies on his way to the Council of Lyons	The Council of Lyons—union of Eastern and Western Church
1276		The second *Roman de la Rose* by Jean de Meung
1277		The condemnation of Averroism and of some theses of Thomas Aquinas
1323	Canonization of Thomas Aquinas by Pope John XXII	

Bibliography of Works of and about St. Thomas

THE MAJOR EDITIONS OF THE WORKS OF AQUINAS

The Leonine Edition (critical Latin text of Aquinas's writings):

Sancti Thomae Aquinatis Opera omnia, published in Rome by a group of Dominican scholars based now at the Priory of St.-Jacques in Paris. Begun in 1882, it currently consists of 28 volumes. This critical edition was undertaken at the order of Pope Leo XIII, from which comes the name "Leonine." Among other works, the Leonine Edition has published the *Summa Theologiae* along with the commentary of Cajetan, and the *Summa contra Gentiles* along with the commentary of Sylvester di Ferrara.

The Paris Edition:

Sancti Thomae Aquinatis Opera omnia (Paris: Vivès, 1871–80) 34 volumes.

The Parma Edition:

Sancti Thomae Aquinatis Doctoris angelici Opera omnia (Parma: Fiaccadori, 1852–73) 25 volumes [Reprint, New York: Musurgia, 1948–50]

ENGLISH TRANSLATIONS OF THE SUMMA THEOLOGIAE

The Summa Theologica, translated by the Fathers of the English Dominican Province (New York: Benziger Brothers, 1947)—reprinted by Christian Classics in five volumes in 1981.

Summa Theologiae (New York and London: McGraw-Hill, 1964–66) 60 volumes: a bilingual Latin/English edition under the general editorship of Thomas Gilby, O.P. These volumes contain valuable introductions and explanatory notes.

ENGLISH TRANSLATIONS OF THE SUMMA CONTRA GENTILES

The Summa Contra Gentiles of St. Thomas Aquinas, literally translated by the English Dominican Fathers from the latest Leonine edition (New York: Benziger Brothers, 1928–9)

    Summa contra Gentiles, translated with an introduction and notes by Anton C. Pegis (Notre Dame, Ind.: University of Notre Dame Press, 1975)

    Some other writings of Aquinas have been translated into English: his commentaries on a number of works by Aristotle, his disputed questions *On Truth, On Power, On Spiritual Creatures,* and *On Charity,* his biblical commentaries on Job, John, Philippians, Ephesians, Galatians, and 1 Thessalonians, and his *Catena Aurea.*

STUDIES ON THE LIFE AND WORK OF AQUINAS

M. D. Chenu, *Toward Understanding Saint Thomas,* translated by A.-M. Landry and D. Hughes (Chicago: Regnery, 1964) which is Chenu's major and magisterial study of the theology and writings of Aquinas.

Thomas F. O'Meara, *Thomas Aquinas: Theologian* (Notre Dame, Ind.: University of Notre Dame Press, 1997)

Jean-Pierre Torrell, *Initiation à saint Thomas d'Aquin:* English translation (Washington, D.C.: Catholic University Press, 1996) which contains a detailed annotated catalogue of the editions of the available works of Thomas Aquinas.

James A. Weisheipl, *Friar Thomas D'Aquino: His Life, Thought, and Work* (Garden City: Doubleday: 1974)

Brian Davies, *The Thought of Thomas Aquinas* (Oxford: Oxford University Press, 1992)

BIOGRAPHIES OF ST. THOMAS

Jacques Maritain, *Angelic Doctor: The Life and Thought of St. Thomas Aquinas* (New York: The Dial Press, 1931)

A. D. Sertillanges, *St. Thomas Aquinas and His Work* (London: Burns, Oates, and Washbourne, 1933)

G. K. Chesterton, *St. Thomas Aquinas* (New York: Doubleday, 1956)

Gerald Vann, *St. Thomas Aquinas* (New York: Benziger Brothers, 1947)

Martin D'Arcy, *Thomas Aquinas* (Westminter: Newman, 1954)

F. C. Coppleston, *Aquinas* (Baltimore: Penguin, 1975)

Joseph Pieper, *The Silence of St. Thomas* (New York: Pantheon, 1957)

Joseph Pieper, *Guide to St. Thomas Aquinas* (New York: Pantheon, 1962)

Martin Grabmann, *The Interior Life of St. Thomas Aquinas* (Milwaukee: Bruce, 1951)

For those who read other languages, an immense bibliography of works about Aquinas exists. See Richard Ingardia, *Thomas Aquinas: International Bibliography 1977–1990* (Bowling Green: Bowling Green State University, 1993). For earlier years, see Vernon Bourke, *Thomistic Bibliography 1920–1940* (St. Louis: Modern Schoolman, 1945), and Terry Miethe and Vernon Bourke, *Thomistic Bibliography 1940–1978* (Westport: Greenwood Press, 1980).

Illustrations

Baudry, Jean, and others, *Bourgogne Romane*. Zodiaque: La nuit des temps 1. Paris: Braun et Cie, 1954. Pages x, 80, 99, 104, 124.

Chenu, M. D., *St Thomas d'Aquin et la théologie*. Paris: Éditions du Seuil, 1959, p. 188. Pages 3, 14, 18, 34, 37, 41, 65, 83, 126, 132.

Dimier, Père M. –Anselme, o.c.s.o., *L'Art Cistercien*. Zodiaque: La nuit des temps, 16. Paris: Cahiers de L'Atelier du Coeur-Meurtry, 1962. Pages 5, 22.

L'Esprit de Cluny. Zodiaque: Les points cardinaux. Paris: Cahiers de L'Atelier du Coeur-Meurtry, 1963. Pages 113, 122.

The St. Louis Art Museum. Page 91

Stahl, Fritz, *Paris: Eine Stadt Als Kunstwerk*. Berlin: Rudolf Mosse Buchverlag, 1928. Page 117.

Tulier, A., *Histoire de Université de Paris et de la Sorbonne*. Paris: Labat (Nouvelle Librairie de France), 1994. Page 73.

Yale University Art Gallery. Page 62.

Index of Names

Index of Subjects

science (of theology), 24–25, 28–29, 117, 137–38

Sentences of Peter Lombard, 53, 135

Summa contra Gentiles, 63f, 136

Summa Theologiae, 29, 44, 54, 71, 97, 98, 137–38

theological virtues, 47, 51, 71

universities, 16

virtue(s), 106f, 112, 118f

vita apostolica, 40, 45